여러분, 수능, 안녕한가요?

쉽고 재미있는 글만 읽을 때는 문제가 없었습니다.
하지만 수능에 출제되는 글을 접하면 상황이 달라집니다.
정답률 34%의 이유, 왜일까요?

그래서 구조독해!

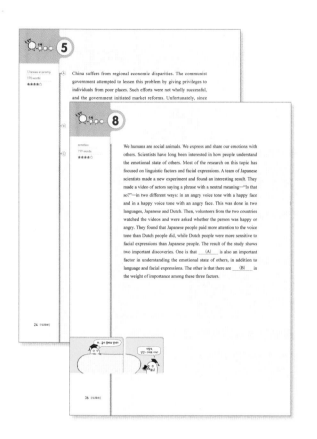

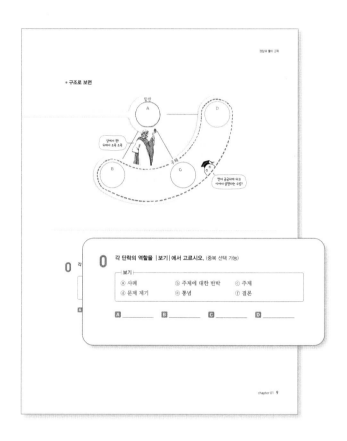

생각을 어떻게 전개했을까?

글쓴이가 자신의 생각을 가장 효과적으로 전달하기 위해 어떤 구조를 선택하고 내용을 전개했을지를 생각하며 읽습니다. 단락으로 나눠진 글에서 시작해서 글 전체를 구조로 읽을 수 있도록 지문이 배치되어 있습니다.

구조로 보면

구조로 글 전체를 보면 글쓴이가 어떤 의도로 단락들을 구성했는지 알 수 있습니다. 0번 문제로 글 전체의 흐름과 단락들의 역할과 관계를 파악했는지 확인할 수 있습니다.

글 전체의 구조　단락의 관계와 역할　각 단락의 핵심 요약

구조독해

영어 독해. 부분에서 헤매지 말고, 글 전체 구조를 보라!

II

디딤돌

독해,
어떻게 하는 거야?

왜냐고?
독해가 안되는 이유는
단어와 문장에만 매달렸기 때문이야!
부분에만 집중하니, 전체가 안 보이지!

구조로 글 전체를 봐!

글쓴이는 글을 쓰기 전에 이런 생각부터 해.
어떻게 하면 내 생각을 가장 효과적으로 전달할 수 있을까?
주제와 생각을 효과적으로 전개하려면 어떻게 설계해야 할까?
설계도를 짜는 이유가 바로 여기에 있어.

그래서 글을 읽을 때
글쓴이가 설계한 구조를 알고 글 전체를 보면
글쓴이가 어디쯤에서 중요한 생각을 말하게 될지,
핵심과 핵심이 아닌 게 뭔지를 구분해내면서
효과적으로 독해할 수 있게 돼.

구조로 글 전체를 봐야 하는 이유야!
글쓴이의 생각을 정확히 볼 수 있으니까!

구조를 봐야 글쓴이 생각이 보인다!

글쓴이가 구조를 먼저 생각했으니까!

왜 구조로 썼을까?

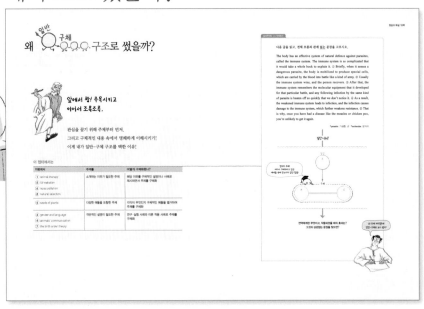

주제를 다루는 글쓴이 의도에 따라
글의 설계도는 달라질 수밖에 없어.
그럼 글이 백 개면 설계도가 백 개냐 그렇지 않아.
검증된 몇 가지 핵심 구조가 있거든.
글쓴이가 어떤 구조를, 왜 선택했는지를 알면
글을 쉽게, 효과적으로 이해할 수 있어.

그래서, 구조로 봐야 한다!

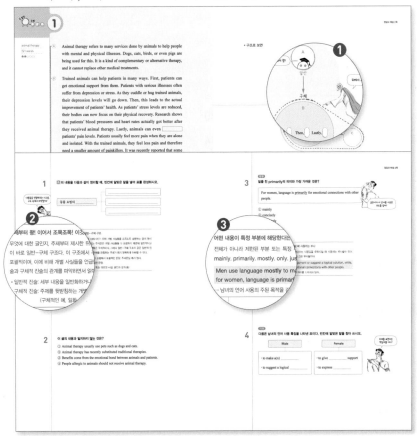

❶ 구조로 보면!
글쓴이의 설계 의도를 따라가면서 단락의 역할과 관계를 파악하다 보면 구조에도 패턴이 있음을 알게 되고, 글을 구조로 보는 습관이 생겨.

❷ 글쓰기 전략을 알면
다양한 전개 방식 속에서 글의 구조와 생각을 효과적으로 파악할 수 있고, 실전에 도움이 되는 팁도 얻을 수 있어.

❸ 어휘 · 어법, 문맥으로 이해하고 쓰임을 알면
글쓴이의 의도와 글의 구조를 효과적으로 파악할 수 있고 문맥 추론능력까지 생겨.

❹ 구조로 글을 보는 나!
제시된 글을 구조로 읽고 흐름을 구분하면서 글쓴이의 생각을 역추적하다 보면 어떤 지문을 봐도 헤매지 않고 글의 요지를 정확히 파악할 수 있게 돼!

부록 단어장

**문맥으로 보고,
반복해서 확인하는 어휘**

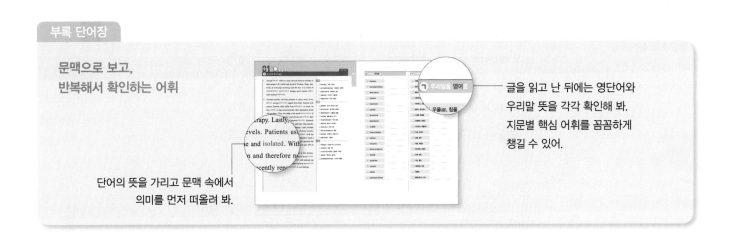

글을 읽고 난 뒤에는 영단어와 우리말 뜻을 각각 확인해 봐. 지문별 핵심 어휘를 꼼꼼하게 챙길 수 있어.

단어의 뜻을 가리고 문맥 속에서 의미를 먼저 떠올려 봐.

구조독해 II

CHAPTER 01 일반 구체

앞에서 쾅! 주목시키고
이어서 조목조목.

CHAPTER 02 판단 근거

판단으로 강하게 단도직입!
탄탄한 근거로 마무리!

CHAPTER 03 구체 일반

이야기로 슬슬 끌어들이고
결론으로 몰아가기!

CHAPTER 04

문제 상황으로 몰아넣고
해결책을 제시!

CHAPTER 05

통념을 꺾고!
내 생각을 주장하기!

CHAPTER

01

일반

구체

앞에서 쾅! 주목시키고 이어서 조목조목.

다음 글을 읽고, 전체 흐름과 관계 없는 문장을 고르시오.

The body has an effective system of natural defence against parasites, called the immune system. The immune system is so complicated that it would take a whole book to explain it. ① Briefly, when it senses a dangerous parasite, the body is mobilized to produce special cells, which are carried by the blood into battle like a kind of army. ② Usually the immune system wins, and the person recovers. ③ After that, the immune system remembers the molecular equipment that it developed for that particular battle, and any following infection by the same kind of parasite is beaten off so quickly that we don't notice it. ④ As a result, the weakened immune system leads to infection, and the infection causes damage to the immune system, which further weakens resistance. ⑤ That is why, once you have had a disease like the measles or chicken pox, you're unlikely to get it again.

*parasite: 기생충, 균 *molecular: 분자의

주제 파악했어?

(A) Animal therapy refers to many services done by animals to help people with mental and physical illnesses. Dogs, cats, birds, or even pigs are being used for this. It is a kind of complementary or alternative therapy, and it cannot replace other medical treatments.

(B) Trained animals can help patients in many ways. First, patients can get emotional support from them. Patients with serious illnesses often suffer from depression or stress. As they cuddle or hug trained animals, their depression levels will go down. Then, this leads to the actual improvement of patients' health. As patients' stress levels are reduced, their bodies can now focus on their physical recovery. Research shows that patients' blood pressures and heart rates actually got better after they received animal therapy. Lastly, animals can even ⬚ patients' pain levels. Patients usually feel more pain when they are alone and isolated. With the trained animals, they feel less pain and therefore need a smaller amount of painkillers. It was recently reported that some patients receiving animal therapy needed only 50% of painkillers.

(C) However, there are some risks involved in this therapy. Those who are allergic to the animals should avoid contact with them. Others who are uncomfortable with animals can get more stress. Sometimes, a patient becomes too attached to an animal, leading to possessiveness or hurt feelings.

● **구조로 보면**

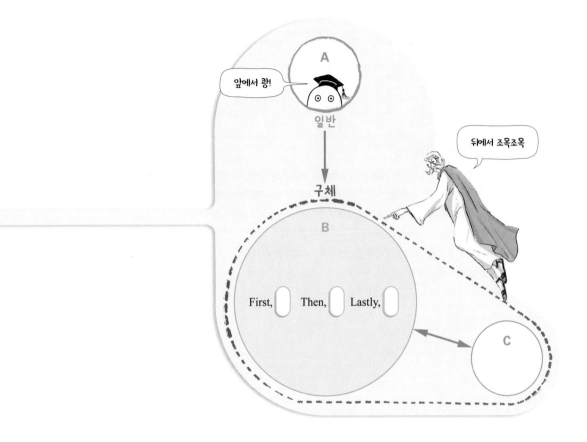

0 각 단락의 내용을 │보기│에서 고르시오.

│ 보기 │

ⓐ benefits of animal therapy

ⓑ definition of animal therapy

ⓒ potential risks of animal therapy

A _____   B _____   C _____

1

B의 내용을 다음과 같이 정리할 때, 빈칸에 알맞은 말을 넣어 표를 완성하시오.

내용들을 연결해주는 시그널,
구조 속에서 파악했어?

동물 요법의 _____

```
┌─────────────────────────────┐
│  _____│
├─────────────────────────────┤
│  _____│
├─────────────────────────────┤
│  _____│
└─────────────────────────────┘
```

주제부터 쾅! 이어서 조목조목! 이것이 일반-구체 구조

무엇에 대한 글인지, 주제부터 제시한 뒤 그걸 이해시키기 위해 개별 사실들을 조목조목 설명하는 글의 형식이 바로 일반-구체 구조다. 이 구조에서 주제 또는 주제문은 개별 사실들을 다 포함하기 때문에 일반적이고 포괄적이며, 이에 비해 개별 사실들을 언급한 문장들은 구체적이다. 그래서 일반-구체 구조의 글은 일반적 진술과 구체적 진술의 관계를 파악하면서 읽어야 글 전체를 관통하는 주제가 뭔지 명확하게 이해할 수 있다.

• 일반적 진술: 세부 내용을 일반화하거나, 부분을 다 포함해서 포괄적인 문장. 주제문일 때가 많다.
• 구체적 진술: 주제를 뒷받침하는 개별 사실을 언급한 문장.
   (구체적인 예, 일화, 과정, 유래, 비교 또는 대조된 사실, 원인과 결과 등)

2

이 글의 내용과 일치하지 <u>않는</u> 것은?

① Animal therapy usually use pets such as dogs and cats.

② Animal therapy has recently substituted traditional therapies.

③ Benefits come from the emotional bond between animals and patients.

④ People allergic to animals should not receive animal therapy.

어휘

3 다음은 동물 요법에 대해 구체적으로 언급한 부분이다. 빈칸에 들어갈 말로 적절하지 <u>않은</u> 것은?

> As they cuddle or hug trained animals, their depression level will go down. Then, this _____ the actual improvement of patients' health.

① causes   ② interferes   ③ results in   ④ brings about

구조상 어떤 문맥?

어휘

4 이 글의 흐름으로 보아, ☐☐☐에 들어갈 말로 가장 적절한 것은?

> Lastly, animals can even ☐☐☐ patients' pain levels.

① increase
② develop
③ maintain
④ reduce

어법·어휘

5 다음은 이 글의 내용을 요약한 것이다. 본문의 단어를 빈칸에 맞게 바꿔서 내용을 완성하시오.

> Animal therapy helps patients _____ in many ways. They can get mental and physical health benefits. However, some people need to be careful in using this therapy.

> _____

seeds of plants

178 words

★★☆☆☆

(A) A plant makes a new plant by moving its seeds. To produce a new plant, the seed must move to a place where it can sprout.

(B) The farther the seed travels, the better it can grow. Why? If the seed settles nearby its mother plant, it cannot get enough light, water, and nutrients due to competition from other plants.

(C) _____, plants have developed various means of sending their seeds as far as possible. Seed size is the most important factor. Light seeds can easily travel long distances by wind. How about bigger and heavier seeds? Interestingly, some seeds have feathery "parachutes." These parachutes enable the seeds to go longer distances. Obviously, these seeds can travel much farther by taking a parachute ride than by simply floating around at the mercy of the wind. Actually, animals help bigger plant seeds travel the longest distance. Animals eat fruits and digest only the soft parts of the fruits. Then, the hard seeds remain inside the stomach. The animals can go long distances and release the seeds in their wastes.

● 구조로 보면

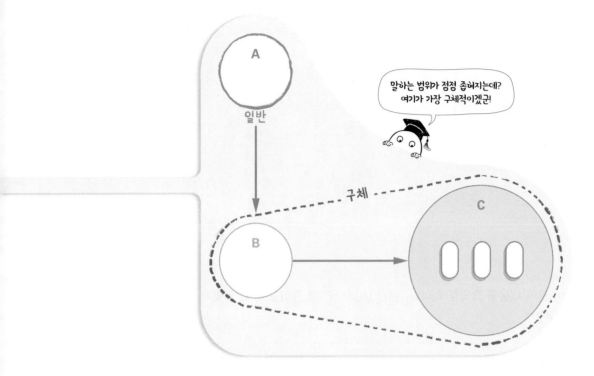

0 각 단락의 내용을 │보기│에서 고르시오.

┤보기├

ⓐ Why do plants spread seeds?

ⓑ How do plants spread seeds as far as possible?

ⓒ Why do plants spread seeds as far as possible?

Ⓐ _____   Ⓑ _____   Ⓒ _____

1

이 글의 흐름으로 보아, 빈칸에 들어갈 말로 가장 적절한 것은?

① In addition
② For example
③ In other words
④ For this reason

2

다음은 이 글의 내용을 요약한 것이다. 빈칸 (A)와 (B)에 들어갈 말로 알맞게 짝지어진 것은?

> Seeds can be _____(A)_____ by various means, such as by wind, by feathery parachutes and by animals, depending on their _____(B)_____.

	(A)		(B)
①	sprouted	………	distance
②	spread	………	size
③	settled	………	nutrient
④	traveled	………	wind

분량은 짧게, 내용은 충실하게! 글의 핵심을 재구성, 요약하기

요약은 단순히 글자 수를 줄이는 것이 아니다. 분량은 짧게, 내용은 충실하게, 글의 핵심을 파악하여 재구성하는 것이다. 주제와 생각을 효과적으로 전달하기 위해 글쓴이가 만들었던 설계도(구조)를 거꾸로 찾아가는 과정과 같다고 할 수 있다. 파악한 글의 구조에 핵심 내용을 얹되, 핵심 내용을 다른 표현으로 바꿔쓰기, 또는 구체적인 내용들을 일반화하여 재구성하면 그것이 바로 '요약'이다. 그래서 요약할 줄 안다는 건 곧 글의 핵심과 구조를 이해했다는 의미나 마찬가지다.

어휘

3 다음은 씨앗을 멀리 퍼뜨리는 이유를 설명하는 부분이다. 빈칸에 들어갈 말로 적절하지 <u>않은</u> 것은?

> 빈칸 앞뒤 내용의 관계는?

> If the seed settles nearby its mother plant, it cannot get enough light, water and nutrients _____ competitions from other plants.

① due to
② owing to
③ because of
④ leading to

어휘

4 밑줄 친 means의 의미와 거리가 <u>먼</u> 것은?

> Plants have developed various <u>means</u> of sending their seeds as far as possible.

① ways
② reasons
③ methods
④ channels

어휘

5 밑줄 친 release의 의미와 가장 가까운 것은?

> The animals can go long distances and <u>release</u> the seeds in their wastes.

① drop
② digest
③ gather
④ cultivate

gender & language

191 words

★★★☆☆

(A) According to linguist Deborah Tannen, men use language mostly to make an argument or suggest a logical solution, while, for women, language is primarily for emotional connections with other people. This difference easily explains why men and women often talk differently in their everyday lives.

(B) First, notice the difference when a sick child approaches her father or mother. When the child says, "Dad, I'm sick. I have a headache," the father's typical response is to say, "Did you take medicine?" to suggest a logical solution. This is sharply contrasted with the mother's typical response, "Oh, dear. Too bad! Let me see how sick you are." Notice that the mother's first response is to express sympathy toward her sick child.

(C) Second, this difference gives us a clue in understanding _____ _____. When a woman says to her boyfriend, "I feel bad about the test result," he often says, "You must change the way you study. Study harder next semester." Then, the woman feels worse than before the conversation, and a heated argument begins. What she wanted was not a solution but sympathy and emotional support.

● 구조로 보면

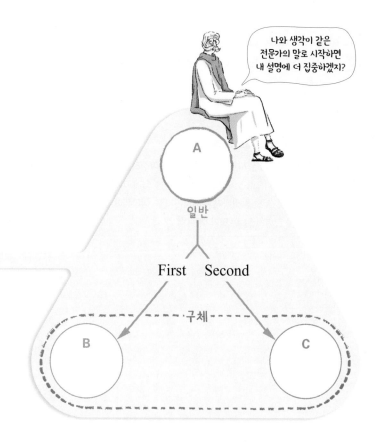

이 글의 주된 서술 방식으로 가장 적절한 것은?

① 문제 해결 사례 제시
② 문제 발생 원인 분석
③ 이론과 반박 이론 대조
④ 예시 속 대조로 이론 설명

1 **이 글의 흐름으로 보아, 빈칸에 들어갈 말로 가장 적절한 것은?**

① why men and women often argue during a date

② how men typically propose to go out with women

③ some physical differences between men and women

④ how men's social behaviors are different from those of women

주제를 선명하게 드러내고 이해시키는 비교·대조 사례

글쓴이가 사례를 비교하거나 대조하는 이유가 뭘까? 각각의 특징을 보여주려는 목적도 있지만, 비교와 대조하는 사례들의 공통점 또는 차이점을 구체적으로 밝혀 독자들이 주제를 쉽게 이해할 수 있도록 하기 위해서다. 따라서 사례가 비교, 대조되고 있다면 '무엇을 말하기 위해서인지'를 생각해야 한다. 글쓴이의 의도를 생각함으로써 글의 주제, 글쓴이의 생각을 분명히 알 수 있기 때문이다.

2 **다음은 이 글의 내용을 요약한 것이다. 빈칸 (A)와 (B)에 들어갈 말로 알맞게 짝지어진 것은?**

일반-구체 구조 속에서 내용을 요약할 수 있나?

> Linguistic research shows that men use language mainly to make a/an _____(A)_____, while women use language mainly to make emotional _____(B)_____. This difference explains why they talk differently every day; in particular, why they often argue during a date.

	(A)		(B)
①	speech	·········	solutions
②	argument	·········	connections
③	harmony	·········	differences
④	decision	·········	expressions

3

어휘

밑줄 친 primarily의 의미와 가장 가까운 것은?

> For women, language is <u>primarily</u> for emotional connections with other people.

글쓴이가 이 단어를 사용한 의도를 알까?

① mainly
② concisely
③ ultimately
④ gradually

어떤 내용이 특정 부분에 해당한다는 점을 가리킬 때 사용하는 부사

전체가 아니라 제한된 부분 또는 특정 부분에만 해당하는 내용임을 주목시킬 때 사용하는 부사들이 있어. mainly, primarily, mostly, only, just 등이 바로 그런 부사들이야.

Men use language **mostly** to make an argument or suggest a logical solution, while, for women, language is **primarily** for emotional connections with other people.

→ 남녀의 언어 사용의 주된 목적을 강조하여 남녀의 차이를 드러내고 있어.

4

어휘

다음은 남녀의 언어 사용 특징을 나타낸 표이다. 빈칸에 알맞은 말을 찾아 쓰시오.

주제를 표현하는 핵심어를 아나?

Male		Female
• to make a(n) _____		• to give _____ support
• to suggest a logical _____		• to express _____

animals'
communication

177 words

★★★☆☆

(A) Like humans, animals can communicate with each other. Studies show that animals such as dogs, cats, elephants, dolphins, chimpanzees, and whales make distinct sounds to send messages. In addition, a recent study shows that some animals can understand and use nonverbal communication.

(B) ⓐ Chimpanzees, for example, can read facial expressions. ⓑ One important characteristic of chimpanzee society is the rank system among its members. ⓒ Researchers showed short videos of positive and negative events to some chimpanzees. ⓓ Then, they showed the chimpanzees images of two facial expressions: positive and negative.

(C) The chimpanzees matched negative facial expressions (such as chimpanzees screaming or showing bare teeth) with photos of animal doctors and needles. ⬜⬜⬜⬜⬜⬜⬜, they matched positive facial expressions with their favorite foods. In other words, the chimpanzees' choices were closely linked with their ability to recognize objects that produce positive and negative emotions.

(D) This research shows that chimpanzees can use nonverbal as well as verbal communication. So, our animal friends are capable of reading the facial expressions of their fellow mates. They might be smarter than we think.

● 구조로 보면

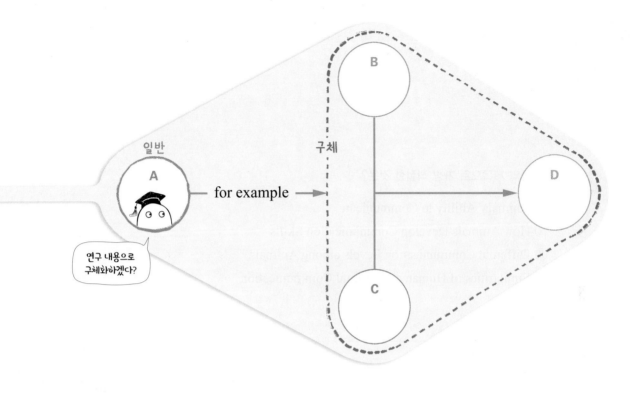

0 각 단락의 역할을 |보기|에서 고르시오.

┤보기├

ⓐ 주제 제시

ⓑ 연구 내용

ⓒ 연구 방법

ⓓ 연구 결과와 해석

A _____   B _____   C _____   D _____

1 다음 중 글의 흐름과 관계 <u>없는</u> 문장은?

① ⓐ   ② ⓑ   ③ ⓒ   ④ ⓓ

이 글의 구조 속에서
다룰 내용이 아닌 것은?

2 이 글의 제목으로 가장 적절한 것은?

① Animals' Ability to Communicate

② How Animals Develop Communication Skills

③ Different Communication Levels among Animals

④ Similarities of Human and Animal Communication

글쓴이가 일관되게 말하는 것!
구조로 보니 헷갈리지 않지?

실험·조사·연구 결과가 곧 글의 주제

객관적인 설명이 필요한 주제일 때 실험·조사·연구 내용을 끌어오는 경우가 많다. 이때 실험·조사·연구의 목적을 언급하거나 결과부터 바로 제시하기도 하는데 이것이 바로 글의 주제이자 요지다. 이어지는 내용은 결과를 증명해주는, 즉 주제를 뒷받침하는 구체적인 사례에 해당하므로 제시된 주제를 염두에 두고 사례를 이해해야 한다.

---

3 이 글의 내용과 일치하지 <u>않는</u> 것은?

① 사람들과 마찬가지로 동물들도 서로 의사소통을 한다.

② 동물 중에는 비언어적인 의사소통을 하는 동물도 있다.

③ 침팬지가 이를 드러냈을 때는 부정적인 감정을 표출하는 것이다.

④ 침팬지가 비명을 지르면 긍정적인 의사 표시를 하는 것이다.

4

어휘

다음 중 nonverbal communication이 <u>아닌</u> 것은?

① gestures
② address
③ eye contact
④ facial expressions

5

어법

이 글의 흐름으로 보아, ⬚에 들어갈 말로 가장 적절한 것은?

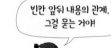

빈칸 앞뒤 내용의 관계, 그걸 묻는 거야!

> The chimpanzees matched negative facial expressions (such as chimpanzees screaming or showing bare teeth) with photos of animal doctors and needles. ⬚, they matched positive facial expressions with their favorite foods.

① Still
② Therefore
③ For example
④ On the other hand

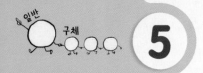

5

(A) What is ultraviolet (UV) radiation? Radiation means the emission of energy, and UV radiation comes mainly from the sun. Most of the UV radiations are blocked by the atmosphere of the earth, and only 2.3% affect us. However, if this small amount of UV rays did not exist, we would not be able to survive.

(B) (①) Without UV rays from the sun, we would not have enough vitamin D, because vitamin D is produced by UV rays. Vitamin D helps to make our bones and muscles stronger. It strengthens our body's immune system and lowers the risk of getting diseases. (②) Also, UV rays kill viruses and bacteria, which helps to keep us healthier. Lastly, vitamin D affects our mood. Sun rays stimulate our brain and produce a certain chemical to improve our mood. (③) If you should live in a region with rainy weather, the lack of UV would often make you gloomy.

(C) (④) Too much UV causes skin cancer and makes you sunburnt. Over-exposure to UV rays could also damage your immune system, and it could harm your eyesight, too. Therefore, you need to protect yourself properly to avoid too much exposure to UV rays.

● **구조로 보면**

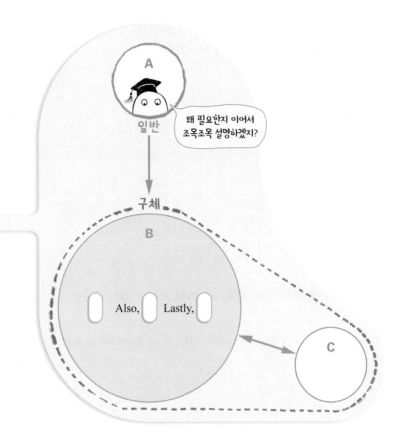

0 **각 단락의 내용을 |보기|에서 고르시오.**

|보기|

ⓐ 자외선의 세 가지 이점

ⓑ 자외선 복사의 정의와 영향

ⓒ 자외선 과다 노출의 위험성

A _____   B _____   C _____

1

일반-구체 구조 속에서,
구체화한 내용을 파악했나?

이 글의 내용과 일치하지 <u>않는</u> 것은?

① 자외선에 의해 비타민 D가 생성된다.
② 비타민 D는 뼈와 근육을 강하게 만든다.
③ 자외선은 살균 작용으로 면역체계를 약화시킨다.
④ 비타민 D는 정서적 도움을 준다.

2

이 글의 흐름으로 보아, 다음 문장이 들어갈 가장 적절한 곳은?

> However, UV rays have negative effects on humans as well.

①   ②   ③   ④

3

글쓴이가 하고 싶은 말,
일반에서 찾고
구체에서 확인했나?

이 글의 요지로 가장 적절한 것은?

① UV rays kill harmful viruses and bacteria.
② UV rays of the sun are beneficial to our mood.
③ We should avoid UV rays as much as possible.
④ A proper amount of UV rays is good for our health.

이 문맥 속에서 쓰인 의미를 아나?

4

어휘

다음은 태양에서 지구로 오는 자외선에 대한 설명이다. 밑줄 친 atmosphere의 의미로 가장 적절한 것은?

> Most of the UV radiations are blocked by the atmosphere of the earth, and only 2.3% affect us.

① the air that you breathe in a place
② the pervading tone or mood of something
③ the envelope of gases surrounding the earth
④ a feeling that a place is pleasant or exciting

5

어휘

이 글에서 사용된 주요 단어들의 관계가 나머지와 다른 것은?

① damage : harm
② stronger : lower
③ produce : make
④ strengthen : improve

6

어법

밑줄 친 which가 가리키는 내용이 무엇인지 우리말로 쓰시오.

> Also, UV rays kill viruses and bacteria, which helps to keep us healthier.

> _____

앞 내용을 이어 설명하는 「콤마(,) + which절」

콤마(,)와 which가 함께 쓰였을 때, which가 앞 문장 전체 내용을 가리킬 때가 있어. 이때 which는 「and + 대명사」와 같고, 앞 문장의 내용을 계속 이어 설명하는 역할을 해.

We didn't attend the meeting, **which** was a big mistake.
= We didn't attend the meeting, **and that** was a big mistake.
우리는 회의에 참석하지 않았고, 그것은 큰 실수였다.

noise pollution

215 words

★★★★☆

(A) Have you ever experienced stress due to loud noises? You are not the only one, and there are many who are suffering various problems due to noise pollution.

(B) Sound is measured in decibels. There are various sounds in the environment, from rustling leaves (20 to 30 decibels) to the wail of an ambulance siren (120 to 140 decibels). Sounds that exceed 85 decibels can harm a person's ears. Noise pollution is any unwanted sound that disturbs the health and well-being of humans and other organisms. It is an invisible danger. It cannot be seen, but it is present, on land as well as under the sea.

(C) Noise pollution affects millions of people on a day-to-day basis. The most common health problem it causes is known as Noise Induced Hearing Loss (NIHL). Exposure to loud noise can also cause high blood pressure, sleep disturbances, heart problems, and stress. Noise pollution impacts not only humans but also wildlife. Loud noises cause insects' hearts to beat faster and birds to have fewer chicks. Animals also use sound for various reasons. [   ], they use sound to direct, to find food, to attract the opposite sex, and to avoid natural enemies. Noise pollution makes it difficult for them to conduct these tasks, which seriously disturbs their ability to survive.

● 구조로 보면

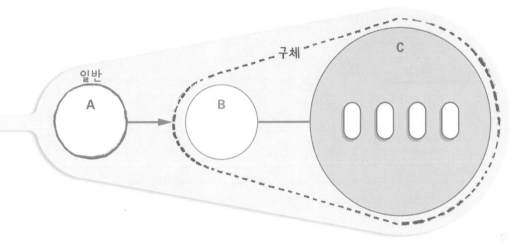

0 **각 단락의 내용을 |보기|에서 고르시오.**

┌─|보기|─────────────────────────────────┐

ⓐ 소음 공해의 정의

ⓑ 소음 공해로 고통받는 사람들

ⓒ 소음 공해가 유발하는 문제들

└──────────────────────────────────────┘

A _____   B _____   C _____

1 C 의 내용을 참고하여 표를 우리말로 완성하시오.

Problems Resulting from Noise Pollution

Humans	소음성 난청, 고혈압, 수면 장애, 심장 이상, 스트레스
Insects	(1) _____
Birds	(2) _____
Animals	(3) _____ (4) _____

구체적 내용을
다 아우르는 일반,
확인했나?

2 이 글의 주제로 가장 적절한 것은?

① the ways to reduce noise pollution

② the various causes of noise pollution

③ the serious influence of noise pollution

④ the socio-economic impact of noise pollution

3

밑줄 친 conduct의 의미와 거리가 먼 것은?

> Noise pollution makes it difficult for them to <u>conduct</u> these tasks, which seriously disturbs their ability to survive.

① do

② perform

③ carry out

④ compete

이 단어로 하려는 말, 파악했나?

4

B에서 noise pollution을 다르게 표현한 말 두 가지를 찾아 쓰시오.

• _____ _____

• _____ _____

주제와 관련된 개념을 다른 표현으로 바꿔쓰는 재진술

글쓴이가 주제를 다룰 때 주요 개념이 무엇인지, 어떤 특징이 있는지, 그것이 미치는 영향은 무엇인지와 같이 다양하게 설명할 때가 있다. 읽는 사람 입장에서는 다른 표현이 계속 등장한다고 느낄 수밖에 없다. 하지만 다 다른 게 아니라 결국 하나를 말하고 있다는 점을 기억하자. 그래서 글을 읽을 때 주제를 파악했다면 그것을 어떤 방식으로 설명하는지 주목해야 한다.

5

이 글의 흐름으로 보아, ⬚에 들어갈 말을 쓰시오.

> Animals also use sound for various reasons. ⬚, they use sound to direct, to find food, to attract the opposite sex, and to avoid natural enemies.

> _____

the birth order
theory

221 words

★★★★★

(A) Many theories in psychology have tried to explain how personality is formed and affected by various factors. The birth order theory, developed by Alfred Adler, an Austrian medical doctor and psychotherapist, is one of them. Adler's birth order theory focuses on the influence of birth order upon the thoughts and behaviors of a child. The theory states that a child's personality traits are not necessarily inherent when a child is born. Instead, the family environment and dynamics between family members, especially the parent-child relationship, play an essential role in shaping a child's personality. For example, an only child tends to receive more attention from parents. This leads to more confidence, self-centeredness, maturity, and sensitivity in the child. As a first child leads younger siblings, the first child tends to be an achiever and leader. Thus, the first child can be controlling, reliable, or protective towards others. As for the second or middle child, the child could be more competitive, rebellious, or independent because the second child should share the attention of their parents with the older siblings.

(C) _____, many studies have stated that the birth order theory exaggerated the effect of birth order on personality. According to other studies, the socioeconomic status of the family, parental attitude, gender roles, and social influences also play a role in forming a child's personality.

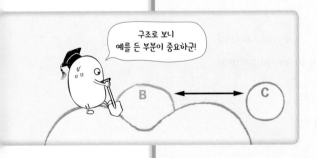

● **구조로 보면**

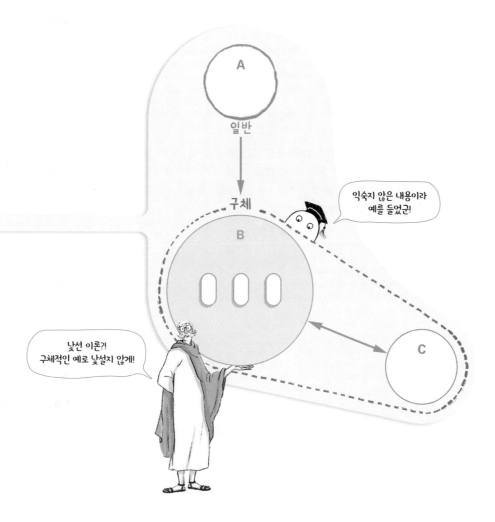

0 이 글을 세 단락으로 나눌 때, B가 시작되는 부분의 첫 두 단어를 네모 안에 쓰고, 각 단락의 역할을 |보기|에서 고르시오.

┤보기├
ⓐ 이론에 대한 소개   ⓑ 이론의 장단점 분석
ⓒ 이론의 문제점 지적   ⓓ 이론에 대한 통념 언급
ⓔ 이론을 설명하는 사례

B [   ]

A _____   B _____   C _____

1 이 글의 흐름으로 보아, 빈칸에 들어갈 말로 가장 적절한 것은?

① However
② Moreover
③ Therefore
④ In other words

내용의 짜임새를 명확하게 만들어 주는 연결어

내용을 논리적으로 연결하거나 흐름을 전환할 때 연결어를 사용하면 문장이나 단락 간의 짜임새가 더욱 명확해진다. 연결어가 빠져 있다 하더라도 내용의 앞뒤 관계를 통해 필요한 연결어를 역추적할 수 있는 것도 글쓴이가 구조 속에서 이미 흐름을 만들어 두었기 때문이다. 글쓴이가 자주 사용하는 연결어를 알고, 내용의 관계를 파악하는 독해 습관이 있다면 글의 흐름과 구조를 쉽게 파악할 수 있다.

· 흐름 전환: but, however
· 결과 제시: therefore, consequently
· 내용 추가: moreover, furthermore, in other words

---

2 다음은 이 글의 내용을 요약한 것이다. 빈칸 (A)와 (B)에 들어갈 알맞은 말을 |보기|에서 골라 문장을 완성하시오.

> Alfred Adler stated that the birth order plays the most important role in _____(A)_____. Nowadays, the socioeconomic status of the family, parental attitude, gender roles, and social influences are also thought to be _____(B)_____ regarding the child's personality.

┌─| 보기 |─────────────────────────
· essential factors
· the effect of birth order
· shaping a child's personality
· explaining a child's inherent personality traits
└──────────────────────────────

(A) _____

(B) _____

3

어휘

밑줄 친 inherent의 의미로 가장 적절한 것은?

> The theory states that a child's personality traits are not necessarily <u>inherent</u> when a child is born.

문맥 속에서 의미를 파악했나?

① in harmonious accordance with nature

② given to someone as a right or privilege

③ slowly developed as the child grows up

④ existing as a natural or basic part of something

4

어휘

이 글에 제시된 다음 단어들을 포괄하는 단어를 B 에서 찾아 쓰시오.

제시된 단어들로 뭘 설명하려는지 알까?

confidence	controlling	reliable
competitive	independent	

> _____

A Have you ever heard of "natural selection"? Natural selection is the process through which species adapt to their environments. Thus, it is the engine of evolution. Charles Darwin, the author of the famous *The Origin of Species*, developed the idea of natural selection.

B Natural selection is the process through which living organisms adapt and change. Individuals in a species are naturally variable. They are all different in some ways. This variation means that certain individuals have traits better suited to the environment than others. Individuals with adaptive traits, that is, the traits that enable certain individuals to adjust better to the environment, are more likely to survive and reproduce. These individuals then pass the adaptive traits on to their offspring. These advantageous traits are transmitted through generations and, over time, become dominant in the population. Then the process of natural selection is completed, and the species adapt successfully to the environment. If the environment changes rapidly, some species may fail to adapt to the change of the environment through natural selection and thus fail to survive. Many fossil records show many of the organisms that once lived on Earth are now extinct. Dinosaurs are one example. Dinosaurs did not have enough time to adapt to the catastrophic change of climate through natural selection, so only their fossils tell that they once thrived on Earth.

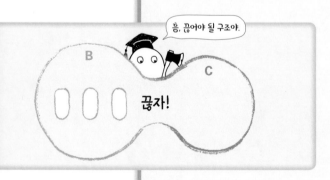

● 구조로 보면

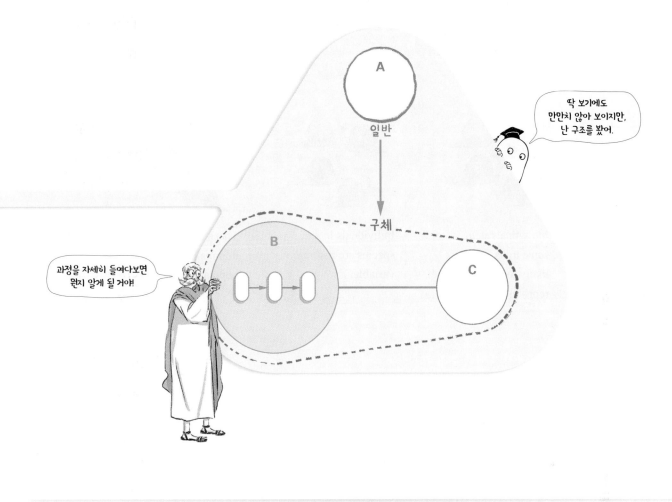

O 이 글을 세 단락으로 나눌 때, **C** 가 시작되는 부분의 첫 두 단어를 네모 안에 쓰고, 각 단락의 내용을 |보기| 에서 고르시오.

┌─ 보기 ┐

ⓐ 자연 선택의 과정   ⓑ 자연 선택의 정의

ⓒ 급격한 환경 변화 과정   ⓓ 환경 적응에 실패한 경우

C [   ]

A _____   **B** _____   **C** _____

이 글의 내용과 일치하도록 제시된 그림을 순서대로 배열하시오.

구조로 내용을 이해했나?

The Process of Adaptation

[　] → [　] → [　]

ⓐ

Individuals with some traits are more likely to survive and reproduce.

ⓑ

Individuals in a species are naturally variable.

ⓒ

These traits become dominant in the population.

2

이 글의 제목으로 가장 적절한 것은?

① The Process of Natural Selection
② The Influence of *The Origin of Species*
③ The Cause of Some Species' Extinction
④ The Environmental Effect on Dinosaurs

3

(어휘)

이 글에서 사용된 주요 단어들의 관계가 나머지와 다른 것은?

① trait : feature
② adapt : adjust
③ pass : transmit
④ dominant : extinct

4

(어법)

다음 두 문장을 참고하여, [   ] 안에서 어법상 알맞은 것을 고르시오.

관계대명사 앞 전치사,
그 쓰임을 알고 있나?

- Natural selection is the process <u>through which</u> species adapt to their environments.
- Many fossil records show many of the organisms <u>which</u> once lived on Earth are now extinct.

(1) You must have some ideas on the subject [which / about which] you are going to write.

(2) This is a matter for them [which / for which] requires further study.

(3) In the past, the port was the window [which / through which] foreign culture came in and spread.

(4) This is the most suitable place [which / on which] to build the new capital.

(5) That failure of the Roman garrison opened a door [which / through which] the Germans invaded the Italian Peninsula.

명사와 관계사절의 의미 관계를 명확하게 보여주는 전치사

명사 뒤에 이어지는 관계사절이 그 명사에 대한 구체적인 정보를 제공한다는 건 알지? 그런데 명사와 관계대명사절 사이에 전치사까지 등장할 때가 있어. 글쓴이는 왜 전치사를 썼을까?

Natural selection is <u>the process</u>. (과정) +
Species adapt to their environments **through** <u>the process</u>. (그 과정을 통해)

→ 두 문장에 공통된 내용이 있으니, 한 문장으로 표현하고 싶었을 거야. 그런데, through the process는 의미상 떼려야 뗄 수 없는 관계! 그래서,

Natural selection is the process **through which** species adapt to their environments.
자연 선택은 과정인데, 그 과정을 통해 종들이 환경에 적응한다는 의미

→ through를 process에 가까이 두어서 그 의미를 분명하게 하려는 의도야.

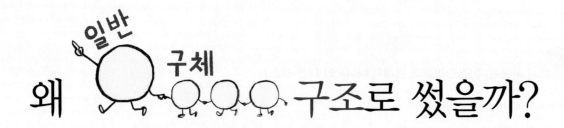

왜 일반 구체 구조로 썼을까?

앞에서 쾅! 주목시키고 이어서 조목조목.

관심을 끌기 위해 주제부터 먼저.

그리고 구체적인 내용 속에서 명쾌하게 이해시키기!

이게 내가 일반-구체 구조를 택한 이유!

이 챕터에서는

지문에서	주제를	어떻게 구체화했나?
① animal therapy ⑤ UV radiation ⑥ noise pollution ⑧ natural selection	소개하는 이유가 필요한 주제	해당 이유를 구체적인 설명이나 사례로 제시하면서 주제를 구체화
② seeds of plants	다양한 예들을 포함한 주제	각각이 무엇인지 구체적인 예들을 열거하여 주제를 구체화
③ gender and language ④ animals' communication ⑦ the birth order theory	객관적인 설명이 필요한 주제	연구·실험 사례와 이론 적용 사례로 주제를 구체화

다음 글을 읽고, 전체 흐름과 관계 없는 문장을 고르시오.

The body has an effective system of natural defence against parasites, called the immune system. The immune system is so complicated that it would take a whole book to explain it. ① Briefly, when it senses a dangerous parasite, the body is mobilized to produce special cells, which are carried by the blood into battle like a kind of army. ② Usually the immune system wins, and the person recovers. ③ After that, the immune system remembers the molecular equipment that it developed for that particular battle, and any following infection by the same kind of parasite is beaten off so quickly that we don't notice it. ④ As a result, the weakened immune system leads to infection, and the infection causes damage to the immune system, which further weakens resistance. ⑤ That is why, once you have had a disease like the measles or chicken pox, you're unlikely to get it again.

*parasite: 기생충, 균 *molecular: 분자의

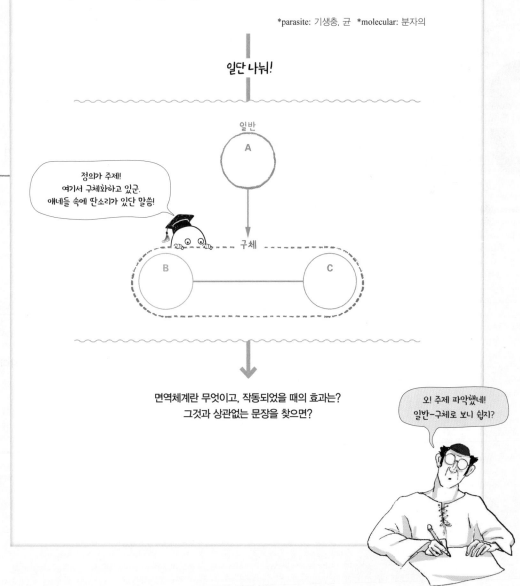

CHAPTER 02

판단

근거

판단으로 강하게 단도직입! 탄탄한 근거로 마무리!

다음 글을 읽고, 밑줄 친 부분 중, 문맥상 낱말의 쓰임이 적절하지 <u>않은</u> 것을 고르시오.

Suspense takes up a great share of our interest in life. A play or a novel is often robbed of much of its interest if you know the plot ① <u>beforehand</u>. We like to keep guessing as to the outcome. The circus acrobat employs this principle when he achieves a feat after purposely ② <u>failing</u> to perform it several times. Even the deliberate manner in which he arranges the opening scene ③ <u>increases</u> our expectation. In the last act of a play, a little circus dog balances a ball on its nose. One night when the dog ④ <u>hesitated</u> and worked with a long time before he would perform his feat, he got a lot more applause than when he did his trick at once. We not only like to wait, feeling ⑤ <u>relieved</u>, but we appreciate what we wait for.

이 글의 구조 속에서, 각 낱말이 글쓴이의 의도에 맞게 쓰였나?

superstitious
beliefs

175 words

★★☆☆☆

(A) Every culture has unique superstitious beliefs. These superstitious beliefs are shared by many people, and often influence their behaviors, including their consumer behavior.

(B) There is an interesting example from Taiwan. Taiwanese people are very sensitive to colors and numbers. For example, for Taiwanese people, the luckiest color is red, and the luckiest number is 8. Taiwanese consumers are more likely to buy a red product than the same item in different colors. Their love of the number 8 is even stronger than that of the color red. They often show a willingness to pay more money to buy a "lucky" number of items inside a package (*e.g.,* 8 golf balls) than the same package with more items (*e.g.,* 10 golf balls). These are examples of superstitious beliefs about colors and numbers.

(C) In this globalized world, the knowledge of superstitious beliefs in different cultures will surely help business people make better decisions. For example, Taco Bell can make much more money by making an eight-layer taco wrap in Taiwan instead of its current seven-layer taco wrap.

● 구조로 보면

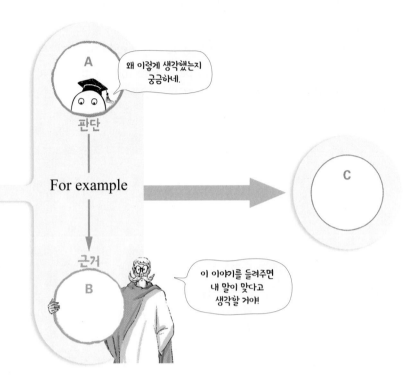

0 각 단락의 내용을 |보기|에서 고르시오.

┤보기├

ⓐ 미신과 인간 행동의 관계

ⓑ 미신의 상업적 활용 가능성

ⓒ 타이완 사람들의 소비 행태

ⓓ 세계화된 미신이 사업에 활용된 사례

Ⓐ _____ Ⓑ _____ Ⓒ _____

1 다음 중 나머지 셋과 성격이 다른 문장은?

① Unique superstitious beliefs often influence people's behaviors.
② For Taiwanese people, the luckiest color is red, and the luckiest number is 8.
③ Taiwanese consumers are more likely to buy a red product.
④ They often show a willingness to pay more money to buy a "lucky" number of items.

2 이 글의 내용과 일치하지 않는 것은?

① 타이완 사람들은 역사적으로 빨간색을 선호해왔다.
② 타이완 사람들의 숫자 8의 선호도는 빨간색에 대한 선호도보다 더 강하다.
③ 한 문화가 갖고 있는 미신적인 믿음은 사업에도 활용도가 크다.
④ 타코벨은 8겹으로 만든 타코를 만들어서 타이완에서 크게 성공하였다.

3 글쓴이가 주장하는 바로 가장 적절한 것은?

① 모든 문화는 미신적 믿음이 유사하다.
② 미신적 믿음이 소비자 행동에 종종 영향을 미친다.
③ 미신적 믿음에 대한 지식은 소비자에게 더 나은 선택을 제공한다.
④ 세계화가 진행됨에 따라 여러 문화의 미신이 모두 획일화되었다.

4

어법

밑줄 친 that이 가리키는 것을 찾아 쓰시오.

> Their love of the number 8 is even stronger than <u>that</u> of the color red.

> _____

같은 말을 반복하지 않으면서 비교 대상을 가리키는 that

글쓴이가 두 대상을 비교할 때 앞에 사용한 명사를 반복하지 않으면서 비교 대상이나 기준을 명확하게 할 때 that을 사용해. (복수형일 땐 those)

<u>Their love of the number 8</u> is even stronger than <u>the color red</u>. (×)
숫자 8에 대한 선호와 빨간색을 비교하는 게 맞을까?

<u>Their love of the number 8</u> is even stronger than <u>that of the color red</u>.
숫자 8에 대한 선호와 빨간색에 대한 선호를 비교해야겠지?

5

어법

다음은 미신의 상업적 활용에 대한 내용이다. 밑줄 친 can의 쓰임을 가장 잘 나타낸 것은?

> Taco Bell <u>can</u> make much more money by making an eight-layer taco wrap in Taiwan instead of its current seven-layer taco wrap.

이 문장의 의도를 알까?

① permission
② obligation
③ possibility
④ necessity

6

어법

밑줄 친 부분 중 어법상 틀린 것은?

① Every culture <u>has</u> unique traditions and customs.
② Koreans <u>are</u> also sensitive to colors and numbers.
③ There <u>are</u> a few interesting examples from around the world.
④ The knowledge of superstitious beliefs <u>are</u> important in business.

2

(A) Icarus is a young man in a Greek myth. Even though only a minor character in the story, his tragic death is a typical example of human folly and has inspired many artists even to this day.

(B) Icarus was a beloved son of Daedalus, a famous inventor of Crete. One day, the King of Crete got angry at Daedalus and imprisoned the father and his son in a dangerous labyrinth. The labyrinth was so fatal that nobody had ever escaped from it. However, it was Daedalus himself that had designed the labyrinth by the King's order. Therefore, he could easily escape from it. However, escaping from Crete was not so easy because Crete was an island. He needed a ship, but no one could take a ship without the King's knowledge. Instead, Daedalus decided to fly in the air. He made wings with feathers and held them together with wax. Before his flight, Daedalus warned his son not to fly too close to the sun, as it could melt the wax in the wings.

(C) At first, their journey on wings was successful, but Icarus got so excited that he forgot his father's warning. He felt very proud of his wings, and he wanted to fly as high as the sun. Eventually, the heat of the sun melted the wax, and young Icarus fell to the sea, to his father's heart-rending grief.

● **구조로 보면**

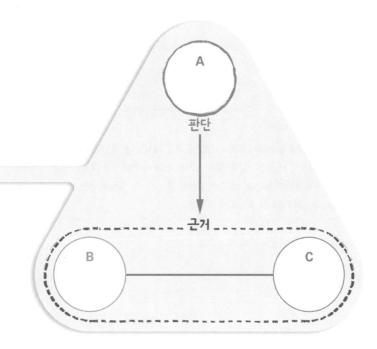

0 **각 단락의 내용을 |보기|에서 고르시오.**

┤보기├

ⓐ 다이달로스의 죽음

ⓑ 이카로스의 자만심과 파멸

ⓒ 그리스 신화와 그 의미 소개

ⓓ 다이달로스와 이카로스의 위기

A _____   B _____   C _____

1

human folly의 의미를 전달하기 위해 글쓴이가 선택한 서술 방식은?

① 등장인물의 일생 소개
② 등장인물 간의 갈등 언급
③ 등장인물들의 성격 대조
④ 등장인물의 행동 진술

이야기 속 등장인물에 주목해야 하는 이유

글쓴이는 읽는 사람들의 동의와 공감을 끌어내기 위해 다양한 근거를 제시한다. 특히 공감대를 넓히면서 자연스럽게 동의를 끌어내기 위해 역사적 사실이나 일화, 널리 알려진 신화 속 이야기를 사용하는데, 이때 중요한 것은 이야기 속 주인공이나 인물들의 행동이다. 왜 그런 행동을 했는지, 그 행동이 어떤 결과로 이어졌는지가 곧 글쓴이가 글을 쓴 목적 즉, 글의 요지에 해당하기 때문이다.

2

밑줄 친 his father's warning이 의미하는 것을 찾아 구체적으로 쓰시오.

> At first, their journey on wings was successful, but Icarus got so excited that he forgot his father's warning.

> _____

3

이 글에 가장 어울리는 속담은?

이 이야기를 소개한 이유?

① Pride goes before a fall.
② It never rains but it pours.
③ A rolling stone gathers no moss.
④ There's no cloud without a silver lining.

어휘

4 밑줄 친 knowledge와 동일한 의미로 사용된 것은?

이 단어가 다양한 문맥 속에서
사용된다는 걸, 아나?

> However, escaping from Crete was not so easy because Crete was an
> island. He needed a ship, but no one could take a ship without the King's
> <u>knowledge</u>.

① The old scholar pursued <u>knowledge</u> to the last day of his life.

② Her vast <u>knowledge</u> of biology was helpful in our joint project.

③ My recent experience made me believe that <u>knowledge</u> is power.

④ It has come to my <u>knowledge</u> that he came back to town secretly.

어휘

5 human folly가 의미하는 구체적인 내용을 우리말로 쓰시오.

folly:
the fact of being stupid,
or a stupid action, idea,
etc.

> Icarus is a young man in a Greek myth. Even though only a minor
> character in the story, his tragic death is a typical example of <u>human
> folly</u> and has inspired many artists even to this day.

> _____

3

Ⓐ Sometimes _____ make the impossible possible. For example, let's take a look at the channel crossing between Britain and France.

Ⓑ Up to 1907, there was only one way to cross the channel between Britain and France. That was, of course, by ship. In 1907, another way was added to the channel crossing: by plane. It was Frenchman Louis Blériot that first flew a plane across the Channel.

Ⓒ In 1994, a third way was added: by undersea tunnel. It is interesting that people thought of constructing an undersea tunnel as early as 1802. A French engineer proposed an undersea highway for horse-drawn carriages in 1802. It is remarkable that people considered it possible to construct an undersea tunnel with the construction techniques of the time. It was in 1987 that the dream began to be realized at last. After the leaders of Britain and France agreed to construct the Eurotunnel, the work finally started. On December 1, 1990, a Frenchman and an Englishman shook hands through a hole connecting the two tunnel ends. It was a memorable day for all who have dreamed of the undersea tunnel between Britain and France.

● **구조로 보면**

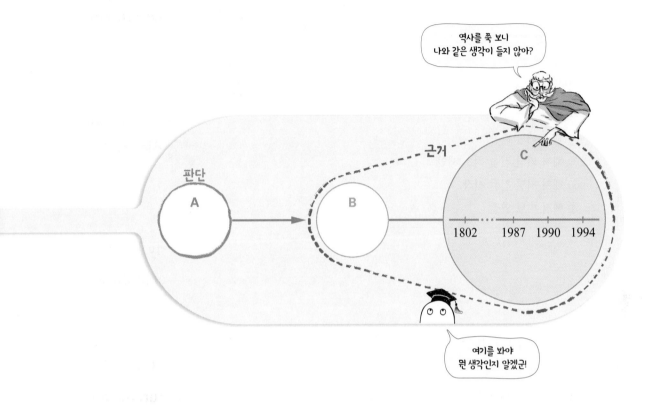

0 각 단락의 내용을 |보기|에서 고르시오.

┌─ 보기 ├─────────────────────────────────
│ ⓐ 해저 터널 완공까지의 과정
│ ⓑ 불가능을 가능으로 만드는 것
│ ⓒ 영국–프랑스 해협을 건너는 두 가지 방법
└──────────────────────────────────────

A _____   B _____   C _____

1 다음은 **C** 의 내용을 시간 순서로 나타낸 표이다. 빈칸에 해당하는 내용을 |보기|에서 고르시오.

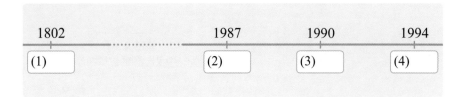

1802	1987	1990	1994
(1)	(2)	(3)	(4)

┤보기├
ⓐ 해저 터널 완공
ⓑ 해저 터널 건설 최초 제안
ⓒ 해저 터널 건설 시작
ⓓ 해저 터널 연결

왜 이런 근거를 제시했는지 알까?

2 이 글의 내용과 일치하는 것은?

① 1994년 이전에는 영국-프랑스 해협을 건너는 방법이 하나였다.
② 영국-프랑스 해협을 건너는 두 번째 방법은 터널을 이용하는 것이었다.
③ 영국인 기술자가 최초로 해저 터널 건설을 제안했다.
④ 최초로 터널 건설을 제안하고 실제로 완공되기까지 오랜 시간과 많은 노력이 필요했다.

3 이 글의 흐름으로 보아, 빈칸에 들어갈 말로 가장 적절한 것은?

① population growth and the need for trade
② peaceful settlements of international disputes
③ economic growth and technological advances
④ ardent wishes, imagination, and strenuous efforts

4

어휘

이 글의 글쓴이가 말한 make the impossible possible의 의미로 가장 적절한 것은?

① creating a product that goes above and beyond expectations

② introducing a new business model that shakes up the market

③ making a new technology that completely changes an industry

④ achieving something that was previously thought to be impossible

5

어법

다음 제시된 문장을 잘못 이해한 사람은?

ⓐ It was Frenchman Louis Blériot that first flew a plane across the Channel.

ⓑ It is interesting that people thought of constructing an undersea tunnel as early as 1802.

ⓒ It is remarkable that people considered it possible to construct an undersea tunnel with the construction techniques of the time.

ⓓ It was in 1987 that the dream began to be realized at last.

① 지우: ⓐ는 비행기로 해협을 최초로 건넌 사람이 누구인지 강조하는 표현이야.

② 유진: ⓑ에서 당시 사람들이 해저 터널 건설 생각에 흥미를 가졌다는 것을 알 수 있어.

③ 미나: ⓒ에서 당시 사람들의 생각에 대한 글쓴이의 판단을 알 수 있어.

④ 승관: ⓓ는 글쓴이가 특정 부분을 강조하면서 사실을 전하는 표현이야.

글쓴이가 특정 부분을 강조하거나 자기 생각을 드러낼 때 사용하는 It ~ that 구문

① 글쓴이가 특정 부분을 강조할 때가 있어. 말로 하면 소리로 강조할 수 있지만 글로 표현할 땐 그에 맞는 형식이 필요해. 그중 하나가 It ~ that 구문이야.

It is a volcanic eruption **that** is the most destructive natural disaster in this area.

→ 다름 아닌 화산 폭발이 이 지역에서 가장 파괴적인 자연재해(글쓴이가 화산 폭발을 강조함)

② 글쓴이가 어떤 내용에 대한 의견이나 판단을 내릴 때가 있어. 이때도 It ~ that 구문을 써.

It is interesting **that** some seeds have feathery "parachutes."

→ 흥미로운 건 어떤 씨앗들이 깃털 모양 '낙하산'을 가진 것(글쓴이가 흥미롭다고 생각함)

4

scientific discovery

202 words

★★★☆☆

(A) Not all scientific discoveries or inventions come from the original plan of scientific researchers. Sometimes they come from mistakes or sheer luck. For example, let's take a look into the case of penicillin.

(B) Since its discovery, penicillin has saved millions of lives. However, its discovery came from a stroke of luck. Alexander Fleming, its discoverer, was looking for ways to destroy bacteria. To do that, he was growing bacteria on laboratory plates. Before going on a holiday in 1928, Fleming made two mistakes. (①) When he came back from his holiday, Fleming noticed that some of his plates were ruined with a fungus, while others were normal. (②) He was about to wash his plates when he found <u>something extraordinary</u>. (③) There were clear spots in the plates where the fungus grew. (④) The fungus had killed the bacteria he was growing! Fleming realized that this might be important, so he labeled and saved the plates. However, Fleming did not succeed in developing medicine from the fungus. It was Howard Florey and Ernst Chain who succeeded in turning the fungus into penicillin. Yet, people will always remember Alexander Fleming as the discoverer of penicillin.

● **구조로 보면**

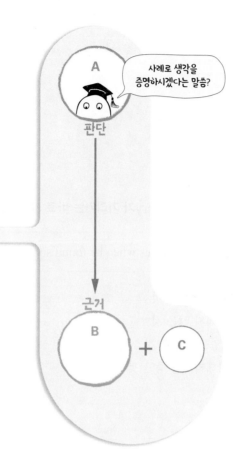

사례로 생각을
증명하시겠다는 말씀?

0 이 글을 세 단락으로 나눌 때, **C** 가 시작되는 부분의 첫 두 단어를 네모 안에 쓰고,
각 단락의 내용을 |보기|에서 고르시오.

┤ 보기 ├

ⓐ 과학적 발견과 발명의 우연성

ⓑ 페니실린 발견자로 기억되는 플레밍

ⓒ 곰팡이를 페니실린으로 바꾼 플레밍

ⓓ 실수로 인해 곰팡이를 발견한 플레밍

C ☐☐☐☐☐☐☐☐☐☐☐☐☐☐☐☐

A _____   **B** _____   **C** _____

1

제시된 이야기 속 틈을 봤나?

이 글의 흐름으로 보아, 다음 문장이 들어갈 가장 적절한 곳은?

> He didn't sterilize his plates, and he left the lab windows open.

①   ②   ③   ④

2

B의 something extraordinary가 가리키는 바로 가장 적절한 것은?

> He was about to wash his plates when he found something extraordinary.

① 실험 접시에 곰팡이가 생긴 것
② 실험 접시가 멸균되지 않은 것
③ 플레밍이 페니실린을 발견한 것
④ 어떤 곰팡이가 박테리아를 죽인 것

3

이 글의 판단과 근거를
모두 반영한 제목은?

이 글의 제목으로 가장 적절한 것은?

① The Effects of Penicillin
② A Mistake that Saved Lives
③ The Necessity of a Mistake
④ Difficulties of Developing Medicine

함축적이거나 상징적인 제목

글의 제목을 정할 때 주제가 곧 제목인 경우도 있지만. 주제에 대한 글쓴이의 생각이나 결론 등을 반영한 함축적인 제목을 붙이기도 한다. 이런 제목은 주제를 포함하면서 보다 큰 개념을 보여주기도 하고 상징적이어서 독자들의 호기심과 관심을 집중시킬 수 있다. 어떤 접근이 되었든 제목은 글의 내용과 글쓴이의 의도를 정확히 반영하는 게 기본이므로, 제목을 판단할 때 글쓴이의 의도에서 벗어나지 않으면서 내용을 충실하게 반영한 제목인지 따져봐야 한다.

4 어법

두 문장의 형식에 유의하여 각각의 의미를 쓰시오.

문장 형식에 담긴 의미를 알까?

> (1) Not all scientific discoveries or inventions come from the original plan of scientific researchers.
> (2) None of the scientific discoveries or inventions come from the original plan of scientific researchers.

(1) _____

(2) _____

글쓴이가 예외적인 상황을 주목할 때 사용하는 부분 부정

부정어와 전체를 의미하는 표현을 함께 사용하면 글쓴이가 전체가 아닌 예외에 주목하고 있다는 뜻이야.
글쓴이가 무엇에 관심을 두고 있는지 알 수 있는 단서가 되니까 이어지는 내용을 주목해서 읽어야 해.

부정어 +	all / every / both	→	모두 / 둘 다	~ 것은 아닌
	always / necessarily / completely		항상 / 반드시	
none / neither		→	전체를 부정	

---

5 어휘

이 글에서 플레밍의 the original plan에 해당하는 것을 |보기|에서 모두 고르시오.

> Not all scientific discoveries or inventions come from the original plan of scientific researchers.

┤보기├

ⓐ looking for ways to destroy bacteria

ⓑ growing bacteria

ⓒ finding a fungus killing the bacteria

ⓓ developing medicine from the fungus

> _____

왜  구조로 썼을까?

판단으로 강하게 단도직입!
탄탄한 근거로 마무리!

강력한 주장부터 먼저!

그리고 타당한 근거로 설득하기!

이게 내가 판단–근거 구조를 택한 이유야.

이 챕터에서는

지문에서	판단을	어떻게 증명했나?
① superstitious beliefs	현상에 대한 해석	현상을 구체적인 사례로
② Icarus	인물에 대한 평가	신화 속 인물의 행동으로
③ undersea tunnel	태도나 가치	실제 사례로
④ scientific discovery	사실에 대한 판단	실제 사례로

다음 글을 읽고, 밑줄 친 부분 중, 문맥상 낱말의 쓰임이 적절하지 <u>않은</u> 것을 고르시오.

Suspense takes up a great share of our interest in life. A play or a novel is often robbed of much of its interest if you know the plot ① <u>beforehand</u>. We like to keep guessing as to the outcome. The circus acrobat employs this principle when he achieves a feat after purposely ② <u>failing</u> to perform it several times. Even the deliberate manner in which he arranges the opening scene ③ <u>increases</u> our expectation. In the last act of a play, a little circus dog balances a ball on its nose. One night when the dog ④ <u>hesitated</u> and worked with a long time before he would perform his feat, he got a lot more applause than when he did his trick at once. We not only like to wait, feeling ⑤ <u>relieved</u>, but we appreciate what we wait for.

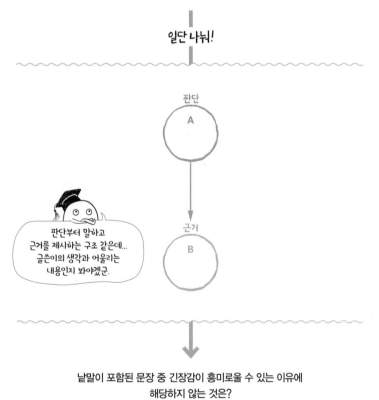

일단 나눠!

판단

A

근거

B

판단부터 말하고
근거를 제시하는 구조 같은데…
글쓴이의 생각과 어울리는
내용인지 봐야겠군.

낱말이 포함된 문장 중 긴장감이 흥미로울 수 있는 이유에
해당하지 않는 것은?

판단-근거 구조로 읽고,
낱말의 쓰임이 글쓴이의 의도와 같은지
제대로 파악했군!

CHAPTER 03

구체

일반

이야기로 슬슬 끌어들이고 결론으로 몰아가기!

주어진 글 다음에 이어질 글의 순서로 가장 적절한 것을 고르시오.

Consider the story of two men quarreling in a library. One wants the window open and the other wants it closed. They argue back and forth about how much to leave it open: a crack, halfway, or three-quarters of the way.

(A) The librarian could not have invented the solution she did if she had focused only on the two men's stated positions of wanting the window open or closed. Instead, she looked to their underlying interests of fresh air and no draft.

(B) After thinking a minute, she opens wide a window in the next room, bringing in fresh air without a draft. This story is typical of many negotiations. Since the parties' problem appears to be a conflict of positions, they naturally tend to talk about positions—and often reach an impasse.

(C) No solution satisfies them both. Enter the librarian. She asks one why he wants the window open: "To get some fresh air." She asks the other why he wants it closed: "To avoid a draft."

*draft: 외풍 *impasse: 막다름

① (A) − (C) − (B)
② (B) − (A) − (C)
③ (B) − (C) − (A)
④ (C) − (A) − (B)
⑤ (C) − (B) − (A)

이 글의 구조 속에서, 내용의 흐름을 파악할 수 있나?

(A) ⓐ The Holocaust refers to the mass murder that happened from 1933 to 1945. During this time, Jews in Europe suffered terribly. Six million Jews were killed, and one-fourth of them were children. As approximately 9 million Jews lived in Europe before the Holocaust, two-thirds of the whole Jewish population in Europe were killed by the Nazis. It is one of the largest mass murders in history.

(B) However, what makes it more meaningful today is the effort to _____ it. ⓑ There are numerous Holocaust memorials and museums throughout the world. They have been built to preserve the memory of the dead and to provide historical knowledge to people of today. Also, many institutions around the world are teaching the Holocaust to the new generations. These are parts of the effort to learn from history.

(C) ⓒ History will repeat itself if we should forget its lesson. Another holocaust could happen if we close our eyes to the tragedy of the Holocaust. Think of those millions of lives who could have lived happily if they [_____]. ⓓ Many of them could have made great contributions to humankind!

● 구조로 보면

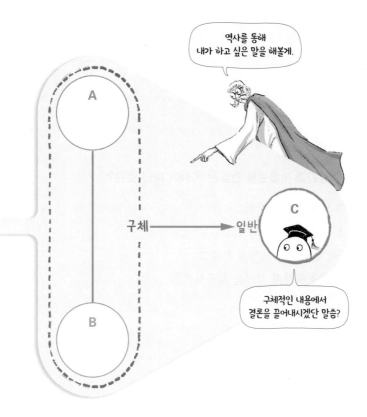

0 이 글에서 글쓴이가 말하고자 하는 바가 가장 잘 드러난 문장을 찾고,
알맞은 말을 넣어 주제를 완성하시오.

① ⓐ　　　　　② ⓑ　　　　　③ ⓒ　　　　　④ ⓓ

주제: learning a ＿＿＿＿＿＿ from history

1

글쓴이가 이 역사 속 이야기를 보여주는 의도는?

이 글의 흐름으로 보아, B 의 빈칸에 알맞은 말을 쓰시오.

> _____

2

홀로코스트 기념관과 박물관을 건립한 목적이 <u>아닌</u> 것은?

① 역사를 통해 교훈을 얻으려고
② 학살의 희생자들을 기억하려고
③ 피해자들에게 물질적 보상을 하려고
④ 젊은 세대에게 역사적 지식을 제공하려고

3

이 글에 가장 어울리는 격언은?

① Difficulty is the excuse history never accepts.
 – Edward R. Murrow

② History is the version of past events that people have decided to agree upon.
 – Napoleon Bonaparte

③ Those who do not remember the past are condemned to repeat it.
 – George Santayana

④ History never looks like history when you are living through it.
 – John W. Gardner

excuse
변명, 구실, 나쁜 사례
condemn
(좋지 않은 상황에) 처하게 만들다

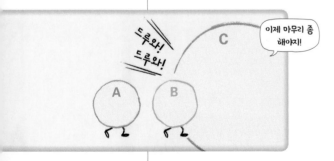

4

어법

다음 문장이 의도하는 바를 고려할 때, ☐☐☐☐☐에 들어갈 말로 가장 적절한 것은?

이 문맥에 알맞은 표현은 아냐?

> Think of those millions of lives who could have lived happily if they
> ☐☐☐☐☐☐☐. Many of them could have made great
> contributions to humankind!

① were not killed
② will not be killed
③ should not be killed
④ had not been killed

돌이킬 수 없는 과거 사실에 대한 유감과 아쉬움을 표현하는 가정법 과거완료

실제 있었던 일을 반대로 가정하여 돌이킬 수 없는 결과에 대한 안타까움과 유감을 표현할 때 가정법 과거완료형을 사용해. 가정법으로 표현된 상황이 실제가 아닌 가정이기 때문에 거리감을 두기 위해 실제보다 더 이전 시제를 써서 표현하는 거야.

> If + 주어 + had p.p ~, 주어 + would/could + have p.p ...
> If I had had enough time, I could have seen more of London.
> 시간이 충분했더라면, 나는 런던을 더 볼 수 있었을 텐데.
> → 시간이 충분하지 않아서 런던을 더 못 봤던 것에 대한 아쉬움을 반대로 가정해서 표현

5

어법

다음은 어떤 글의 일부이다. 문맥으로 보아, ☐☐☐☐☐ 안에서 어법상 알맞은 것을 고르시오.

> The Nobel Prize-winning biologist Peter Medawar said that about four-fifths of his time in science was wasted, adding sadly that "nearly all scientific research leads nowhere." What kept all of these people going when things were going badly was their passion for their subject. Without such passion, they would achieve / have achieved nothing.
>
> − 고1 기출 −

실제 있었던 일을 반대로 가정하여 그 일의 의미를 되짚어 볼 때 사용하는 가정법

► p.141 참조

2

broken windows theory

198 words

★★★☆☆

(A) In the past, New York City subways were dangerous. They were filthy, outdated, and poorly maintained, and New Yorkers feared that they would be a target of crime. Train cars and the subway stations were also covered with graffiti.

(B) In the 1980s, New York City began to clean up its subway stations and subway cars. Day after day, the city cleaned up graffiti, yet new graffiti appeared overnight. However, the city did not give in, and continued its cleanup efforts. (①) The graffiti gradually disappeared, and the crime rate in New York subways also dropped by 75%.

(C) (②) This was a classic example of the "broken windows theory." (③) According to the theory, small signs of disorder — graffiti, dirty streets, or broken windows — lead to more serious disorders, such as murder, robbery, or drug-related crime. (④) New York police realized that stopping small crimes helped prevent bigger crimes, so they began to enforce tough laws against petty crimes.

(D) This significantly decreased the city's crime rate. Reducing crime using the "broken windows theory" resulted in quick change with minimal cost. Now, many cities in America follow New York City's example to protect their citizens.

● **구조로 보면**

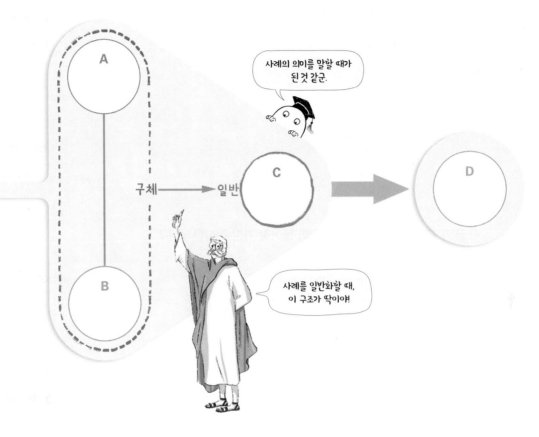

○ **각 단락의 내용을 |보기|에서 고르시오.**

┌ |보기| ┐

ⓐ What was the outcome?

ⓑ What was the problem?

ⓒ What was the basis of the action?

ⓓ What action was taken to solve the problem?

└ ┘

A _____ **B** _____ **C** _____ **D** _____

1 **이 글의 구조를 가장 잘 설명한 것은?**

① 사례들과 반박 이론
② 사례들과 유사 사례 비교
③ 문제 해결 사례와 이론적 설명
④ 사례들의 인과 관계와 문제 제기

2 **이 글의 흐름으로 보아, 다음 문장이 들어갈 가장 적절한 곳은?**

> What was the outcome of the cleanup?

①　　　　　②　　　　　③　　　　　④

3 **뉴욕시의 치안이 크게 향상된 이유로 가장 적절한 것은?**

이 글의 구조를 보며 내용을 잘 파악하고 있나?

① 뉴욕시의 지하철 낙서를 모두 지웠기 때문에
② 도시의 깨진 유리창을 모두 보수했기 때문에
③ 뉴욕시 당국이 경범죄도 엄벌에 처했기 때문에
④ 뉴욕시 당국이 중범죄에 대한 형벌을 강화했기 때문에

사례에서 끌어낸 결론이 글의 요지

글쓴이가 글을 전개할 때 자신의 의견을 먼저 밝히기도 하지만, 구체적인 이야기나 실제 사례를 먼저 제시해서 읽는 이들의 흥미와 관심부터 끌어내는 방식을 쓰기도 한다. 사례가 어떤 것이든 그것은 반드시 글쓴이의 결론으로 이어지게 된다. 사례를 읽을 때 사건의 인과 관계 또는 담긴 메시지를 생각하면서 읽어야 하는 이유다.

어휘

4 단어들의 관계가 나머지와 <u>다른</u> 것은?

① filthy : dirty

② tough : strict

③ petty : serious

④ classic : typical

어휘

5 다음은 '깨진 창문 이론'을 설명한 내용이다. 빈칸에 들어갈 말로 가장 적절한 것은?

> This was a classic example of the "broken windows theory." According to the theory, small signs of disorder — graffiti, dirty streets, or broken windows — _____ more serious disorders, such as murder, robbery, or drug-related crime.

사례에 해당하는 원리나 효과를 제시할 때 사용하는 신호

This is/was an example of the 원리 또는 효과.

이 글의 구조 속에서 문맥을 파악했나?

① rely on

② result in

③ stand for

④ begin with

Clyde Tombaugh

232 words

★★★☆☆

Clyde Tombaugh

Tombaugh Regio

Ⓐ Pluto was discovered by Clyde Tombaugh. Tombaugh was not a trained scientist. In fact, he started life as a farmer, and made his own telescopes using scraps from agricultural equipment. In his early 20s, he contacted the Lowell Observatory to ask for feedback on his work. The observatory was so impressed with his drawings of Mars and Jupiter that it offered to hire him. Working as an assistant, he discovered Pluto and ⓐ its moon Charon in 1930.

Ⓑ Eighty years after ⓑ its discovery, we finally have an up-close view of Pluto. Launched in 2006, NASA's space probe "New Horizons" has sent us a photo which clearly shows a heart-shaped region of Pluto, named "Tombaugh Regio" after ⓒ its discoverer.

Ⓒ Inside the space probe was placed a small container holding Tombaugh's ashes, in honor of Tombaugh's last wishes to have his ashes sent to Pluto. (①) ⓓ Its cargo also carried a coin. (②) In Greek mythology, Pluto is the god of the underworld, and Charon is the old man who helps the dead cross the river Styx. (③) Scientists at NASA added a quarter to wish Tombaugh a safe journey to the underworld. (④)

Ⓓ A speck of light, first discovered by a farmer-turned-scientist, is now better defined and better understood thanks to state-of-the-art technology. Now, New Horizons is on a new mission to another unknown region, the Kuiper Belt.

*the Kuiper Belt: 해왕성 바깥쪽에서 태양의 주위를 돌고 있는 작은 천체들의 집합체

● **구조로 보면**

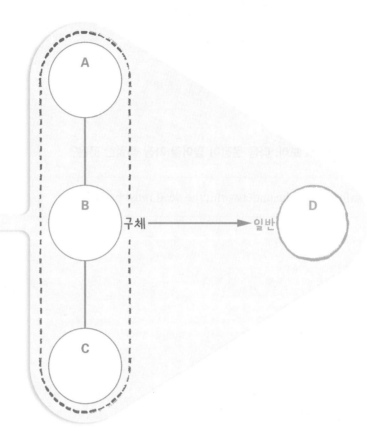

0 **각 단락의 내용을 |보기|에서 고르시오.**

> **|보기|**
>
> ⓐ 탐사선으로 명왕성에 보낸 화물
>
> ⓑ 탐사선이 명왕성에서 전송해 온 사진
>
> ⓒ 탐사선의 역할과 새로운 임무
>
> ⓓ 명왕성을 발견한 과학자

A _____   B _____   C _____   D _____

밑줄 친 부분이 가리키는 대상이 나머지와 다른 것은?

구체적 내용을 파악하려면,
가리키는 대상을 알아야 할걸?

① ⓐ   ② ⓑ   ③ ⓒ   ④ ⓓ

이 글의 흐름으로 보아, 다음 문장이 들어갈 가장 적절한 곳은?

> To safely reach the underworld, the dead must pay Charon.

①   ②   ③   ④

이 글의 내용과 일치하는 것은?

① 톰보는 명왕성을 발견했을 당시 저명한 천문학자였다.
② 톰보는 로웰 천문대 재직 당시 망원경을 직접 제작하였다.
③ 톰보는 명왕성의 하트 모양 지형을 처음으로 발견했다.
④ 톰보는 화장한 자신의 유골을 명왕성으로 보내 달라는 유언을 남겼다.

이 글을 쓴 목적으로 가장 적절한 것은?

구체-일반 구조로
이 글을 쓴 이유를 아나?

① 명왕성 탐사의 역사를 알려주기 위해
② 사례를 통해 우주탐사의 어려움을 전달하기 위해
③ 명왕성을 발견한 인물과 명왕성 탐사를 소개하기 위해
④ 신화를 통해 명왕성이라는 이름의 유래를 설명하기 위해

5

어휘

빈칸에 알맞은 말을 |보기|에서 골라 문장을 완성하시오.

| 보기 |

part-time   case-by-case   up-to-date   out-of-date

salt-and-pepper   out-of-work   brand-new

(1) I traded in my second-hand car for a(n) ＿＿＿＿＿＿ one.

(2) He's a(n) ＿＿＿＿＿＿ actor. He can't find any acting opportunities.

(3) ＿＿＿＿＿＿ hair is a natural part of the aging process.

(4) It's a(n) ＿＿＿＿＿＿ guidebook. The information is old.

여러 단어를 연결해 한 단어를 만드는 하이픈(hyphen)

여러 단어를 묶어서 하나의 의미를 만들 때 하이픈을 사용하며, 본문에 나온 것처럼 합성어 또는 형용사 역할을 하지. 하이픈을 사용하게 되면 문장이 간결해져서 가독성이 높아져.

- an **up-close** view of Pluto   명왕성을 아주 가까이에서 보기
- a **heart-shaped** region of Pluto   명왕성의 하트모양의 지역
- a **farmer-turned-scientist**   농부 출신 과학자
- **state-of-the-art** technology   최첨단 기술

6

어법

＿＿＿＿ 안에서 어법상 알맞은 것을 고르시오.

(1) ⌈ Inviting / Invited ⌋ to a dinner party, we feel under pressure to invite our hosts to one of ours.

(2) ⌈ Wanting / Wanted ⌋ to honor as well as observe him, the villagers prepared a banquet.

(3) Only in terms of the physics of image formation ⌈ do / does ⌋ the eye and camera have anything in common.

(4) At the root of trained incapacity ⌈ is / are ⌋ a job with little variety and repetitive tasks.

문맥에 맞게
단어를 사용할 수 있나?

Claude Cassirer could hardly believe his eyes as he stared at a photo of Camille Pissarro's "A Rainy Afternoon in Paris." The picture which hung in a Spanish museum was taken from his grandmother's house by the Nazis during World War II. Claude came from a prosperous Jewish family in Germany. When WW II broke out, persecution of Jews began, and Claude's grandparents applied for an exit visa. (①) The Nazis told them that they could leave Germany, but they could not take the painting with them. (②) If they refused, they would end up in a concentration camp. (③) Since then the picture changed hands at least five times traveling through three countries. (④) Claude asked the museum to return the painting. But the museum refused, so he sued for its return. Cassirer said, "The picture is a stolen property. It should be returned to its rightful owner." However, the museum said that it had obtained the picture legally and that it had no reason to return the picture. The case is still undecided. Many works of art such as this Pissarro painting still have not been returned to their original owners. Cases like this masterpiece are forcing us to reevaluate the issue of property, law, and morality.

● **구조로 보면**

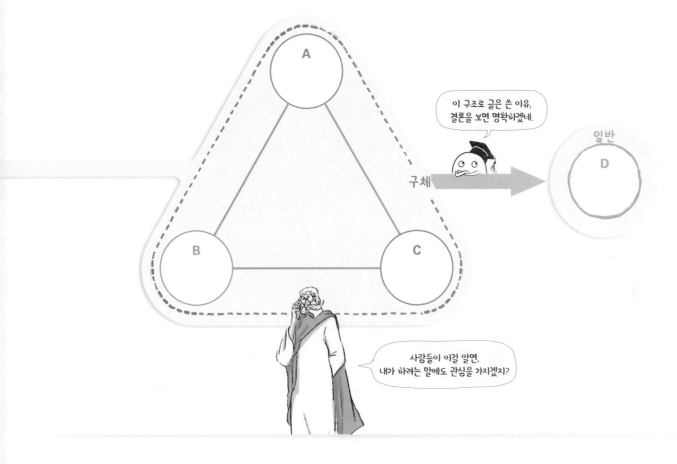

0   이 글을 네 단락으로 나눌 때, 각 단락이 시작되는 부분의 첫 두 단어를 네모 안에 쓰고,
단락의 내용을 |보기|에서 고르시오.

┌─|보기|──┐
│ ⓐ 남겨진 과제   ⓑ 클로드의 요청   │
│ ⓒ 클로드의 발견   ⓓ 클로드 조부모의 과거 상황   │
└──┘

A [Claude Cassirer]   _____

B [   ]   _____

C [   ]   _____

D [   ]   _____

1 이 글의 흐름으로 보아, 다음 문장이 들어갈 가장 적절한 곳은?

> His family left Germany without the picture, and it was considered lost forever.

①   ②   ③   ④

2 이 글의 내용과 일치하는 것은?

① 클로드 카시러는 가난한 집에서 태어났다.
② 클로드 카시러의 조부모는 독일을 탈출하지 못했다.
③ 피사로의 그림은 여러 차례 주인이 바뀌었다.
④ 피사로의 그림은 클로드 카시러에게 반환되었다.

3 이 글의 제목으로 가장 적절한 것은?

① Art Stolen by the Nazis Is Still Missing
② Documenting Nazi Plunder of European Art
③ Dispute Surrounding Ownership of Art Stolen by the Nazis
④ Why It's So Hard to Find the Original Owners of Nazi-Looted Art

Q) 각각의 의미는?
secure ▶
acquire ▶
purchase ▶
obtain ▶

4 〔어휘〕

다음은 카시러와 박물관의 대립되는 입장을 보여주는 내용이다. 빈칸에 들어갈 말로 적절하지 <u>않은</u> 것은?

> Cassirer said, "The picture is a stolen property. It should be returned to its rightful owner." However, the museum said that it had _____ the picture legally and that it had no reason to return the picture.

① secured
② acquired
③ purchased
④ developed

5 〔어법 · 어휘〕

□□□□□ 안에서 문맥상 알맞은 것을 고르시오.

(1) The trees made ⌈ hard / hardly ⌉ any difference in the amount of noise, but they did block the view of the highway.

(2) I am ⌈ hard / hardly ⌉ prepared to answer that question, or even give an opinion regarding it.

문맥에 맞게 단어를 사용할 줄 알까?

---

not 없이도 부정문을 만드는 hardly

언뜻 보면 형용사 hard에 '-ly'를 붙인 부사인 줄 착각하기 쉽지만, hardly는 '거의 아닌'의 뜻으로 부정어나 마찬가지야.

① hardly: 거의 ～없는, 거의 ～아닌, 거의 ～못한

Claude Cassirer could **hardly** believe his eyes as he stared at a photo.
클로드 카시러는 사진을 응시하며 그의 눈을 거의 믿을 수 없었다.

② hard: 열심인/열심히, 힘든/힘들게, 단단한

It is **hard** to believe that he's only six.	믿기 힘든 건 그가 겨우 6살이라는 사실이다.
We have to study **hard** for the final exam.	우리는 기말고사를 위해 열심히 공부해야 한다.

왜 구체 일반 구조로 썼을까?

이야기로 술술 끌어들이고
결론으로 몰아가기 !

공감대를 넓히기 위해 이야기부터 먼저!

그리고 이야기의 흐름을 따라가다 보면

당연해지는 교훈과 결론!

이게 내가 구체–일반 구조를 택한 이유!

이 챕터에서는

지문에서	구체적인 내용을 근거로	어떤 결론을 끌어냈나?
① the Holocaust ④ issue of property	역사적 사건으로	교훈과 시사점
② broken windows theory	사회 현상과 구체적 사례로	사회 심리적 현상에 대한 해석
③ Clyde Tombaugh	특정 분야의 인물 사례로	인물의 의미와 현대에 미친 영향

주어진 글 다음에 이어질 글의 순서로 가장 적절한 것을 고르시오.

> Consider the story of two men quarreling in a library. One wants the window open and the other wants it closed. They argue back and forth about how much to leave it open: a crack, halfway, or three-quarters of the way.

(A) The librarian could not have invented the solution she did if she had focused only on the two men's stated positions of wanting the window open or closed. Instead, she looked to their underlying interests of fresh air and no draft.

(B) After thinking a minute, she opens wide a window in the next room, bringing in fresh air without a draft. This story is typical of many negotiations. Since the parties' problem appears to be a conflict of positions, they naturally tend to talk about positions—and often reach an impasse.

(C) No solution satisfies them both. Enter the librarian. She asks one why he wants the window open: "To get some fresh air." She asks the other why he wants it closed: "To avoid a draft."

*draft: 외풍   *impasse: 막다름

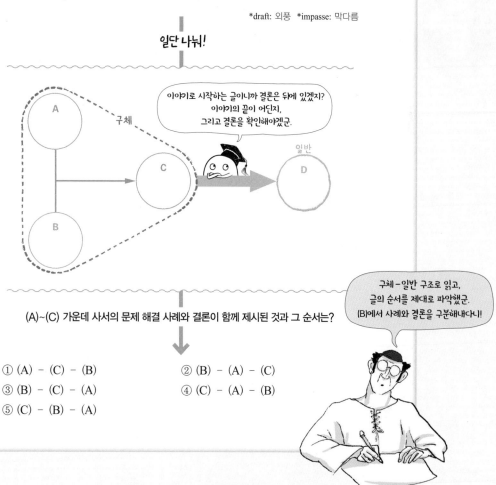

일단 나눠!

이야기로 시작하는 글이니까 결론은 뒤에 있겠지?
이야기의 끝이 어딘지,
그리고 결론을 확인해야겠군.

구체 – 일반 구조로 읽고,
글의 순서를 제대로 파악했군.
(B)에서 사례와 결론을 구분해내다니!

(A)~(C) 가운데 사서의 문제 해결 사례와 결론이 함께 제시된 것과 그 순서는?

① (A) – (C) – (B)   ② (B) – (A) – (C)
③ (B) – (C) – (A)   ④ (C) – (A) – (B)
⑤ (C) – (B) – (A)

CHAPTER

04

문제 해결

문제 상황으로 몰아넣고 해결책을 제시!

다음 글을 읽고, 주어진 문장이 들어가기에 가장 적절한 곳을 고르시오.

Instead of that, say to them, 'I can't deal with that now but what I can do is I can ask Brian to give you a hand and he should be able to explain them.'

Whenever you say what you can't do, say what you can do. This ends a sentence on a positive note and has a much lower tendency to cause someone to challenge it. (①) Consider this situation—a colleague comes up to you and asks you to look over some figures with them before a meeting they are having tomorrow. (②) You simply say, 'No, I can't deal with this now.' (③) This may then lead to them insisting how important your input is, increasing the pressure on you to give in. (④) Or, 'I can't deal with that now but I can find you in about half an hour when I have finished.' (⑤) Either of these types of responses are better than ending it with a negative.

이 글의 구조 속에서,
주어진 문장의 역할을 파악했나?

wrong posture

214 words

★★☆☆☆

(A) We spend a lot of time in front of our desk every day. But your desk isn't built for you only. It's built for anyone. And the wrong posture can lead to aches and pain. So, here are some tips to relieve pain.

(B) First, adjust the height of your chair so that your elbows are bent to 90 degrees. And use a foot stool if your feet don't touch the floor. Next, adjust your monitor. Place the monitor close enough—about arm's length—so that you're able to read without having to strain your eyes or to bend forward to adjust your posture. Also, raise the monitor up until the top of the screen meets eye level. For a laptop, use a stand to raise the screen to the proper height. Then attach an external keyboard and mouse to it. If you work from two monitors, place the primary monitor directly in front of you. If you use both monitors equally, line them up so that you are in the middle of the two. And finally, don't forget to take a break. After 10-15 minutes, we tend to slouch. Learn to stretch while sitting in your chair. Most importantly, get up out of your chair, and move around, at least once an hour.

● **구조로 보면**

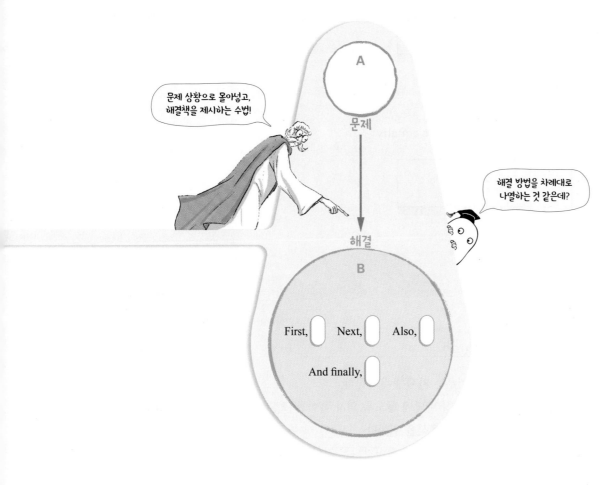

0 **각 단락의 내용을 |보기|에서 고르시오.**

|보기|

ⓐ 통증을 덜기 위한 조언

ⓑ 책상에서의 자세와 통증의 관계

ⓒ 맞춤형 책상의 통증 감소 효과

A _____ **B** _____

1 모니터를 두 대 사용할 때 올바른 나의 위치는?

(1) when monitor 2 is the primary monitor

(2) when you use both monitors equally

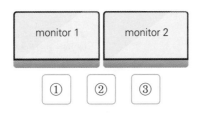

2 이 글의 내용과 일치하는 것은?

① 책상과 상체가 직각을 이루는 자세를 유지한다.
② 의자에 앉았을 때 발이 항상 바닥에 닿도록 의자 높이를 조절한다.
③ 10분에서 15분마다 틈틈이 휴식을 취한다.
④ 최소한 한 시간에 한 번은 일어나서 돌아다니는 것이 좋다.

3 이 글의 주제로 가장 적절한 것은?

① how to avoid injuries at the workplace
② how to find office furniture at a low price
③ how to achieve a successful work-life balance
④ how to reduce pain caused by the wrong posture

어휘

4 밑줄 친 relieve의 의미와 가장 가까운 것은?

So, here are some tips to <u>relieve</u> pain.

① ease
② suffer
③ worsen
④ experience

이 글을 쓴 목적을 아나?

어휘

5 밑줄 친 primary의 의미와 거리가 <u>먼</u> 것은?

If you work from two monitors, place the <u>primary</u> monitor directly in front of you.

① main
② original
③ principal
④ secondary

(A) Have you ever had a song repeated in your mind endlessly, after you accidentally picked it up somewhere else? For example, you hear a tune on the radio on your way to school, and it sticks in your head and repeats itself all day long. Or, you hear a part of an old pop song on the street, and it runs in your head all afternoon.

(B) Actually, this music repetition is so common that almost everyone experiences it from time to time. Women are more sensitive about it, and it lasts longer for them. It may remain for a few days, and it is also highly [_____]. When a person begins to hum the tune, other people can "catch" it, and they may also hum the tune all day long.

(C) This phenomenon is called an "earworm." As you can guess, the name "earworm" comes from the image of a worm living in the ear, thus making the same music again and again in your ear.

(D) Scientists say that an earworm is a kind of brain itch. When people have an itch on their bodies, they scratch themselves repeatedly. Similarly, you catch the repetitive tune, and it will keep on running in your head. If you want to get rid of an earworm, try chewing gum or listening to the song to the end. Trying to find a "cure song" such as the "Happy Birthday" song could help, too.

정답과 해설 42쪽

● **구조로 보면**

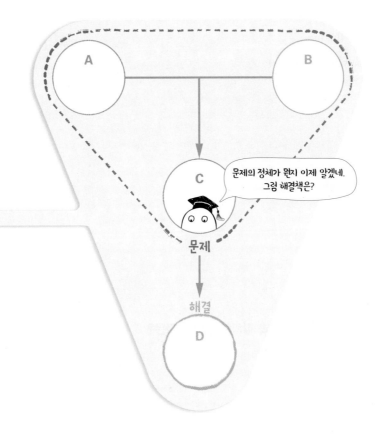

0 각 단락의 내용을 |보기|에서 고르시오.

┤보기├

ⓐ 현상을 가리키는 말   ⓑ 현상의 특징

ⓒ 현상의 경험 사례   ⓓ 현상을 멈추는 방법

A _____   B _____   C _____   D _____

다음에 제시된 표현이 설명하는 것을 찾아 쓰시오.

여러 표현으로 주제를 반복해서 보여주고 있단 걸 아나?

> • had a song repeated in your mind endlessly
> • sticks in your head
> • hum the tune
> • a kind of brain itch

> ＿＿＿＿＿＿＿＿＿＿＿＿

2 earworm에 대한 내용과 일치하지 <u>않는</u> 것은?

① 타인에게 전염된다.
② 뇌에서 발생한다.
③ 가려움증을 동반한다.
④ 껌을 씹으면 없어질 수 있다.

3 이 글의 제목으로 가장 적절한 것은?

① The Influence of Earworms on Women
② The Cure and Side Effects of Earworms
③ The Symptoms and Remedy of Earworms
④ The Difference Between an Itch and an Earworm

4

어휘

밑줄 친 tune의 의미와 가장 가까운 것은?

> For example, you hear a <u>tune</u> on the radio on your way to school, and it sticks in your head and repeats itself all day long.

① noise

② rumor

③ request

④ melody

5

어휘

이어지는 내용으로 보아, ⬚에 들어갈 말로 가장 적절한 것은?

> It may remain for a few days, and it is also highly ⬚.
> When a person begins to hum the tune, other people can "catch" it, and they may also hum the tune all day long.

① infectious

② interesting

③ dangerous

④ comfortable

Emma

214 words

★★☆☆☆

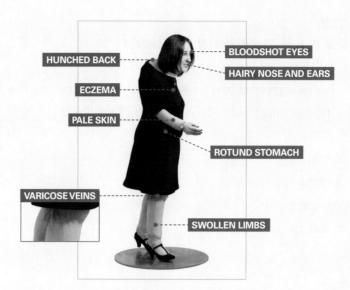

HUNCHED BACK

BLOODSHOT EYES

HAIRY NOSE AND EARS

ECZEMA

PALE SKIN

ROTUND STOMACH

VARICOSE VEINS

SWOLLEN LIMBS

(A) Emma is an image of an office worker who has had unhealthy office behavior and defective office equipment for over 20 years. As you can see in the illustration, Emma is stooped and sallow-skinned. Also, she has dry, red eyes and swollen wrists and ankles. These ailments are caused by sitting long hours in a bad position, too much staring at the computer screen, lack of sun rays, or poor air quality in the office.

(B) Emma, 'The Work Colleague of the Future' campaign, was developed by UK researchers to warn people of the danger of poor posture and inadequate office environment. We sit still at our desks too long without moving, and our bodies are impacted by this lifestyle. It is not just muscles and bones that are damaged. Diseases such as heart problems, diabetes, and even cancer can be accelerated.

(C) Not to become Emma, we should better consider our well-being at work. We should avoid sitting for long hours without changing positions. We need to take regular breaks and move as much as possible during working hours. As for the employers, they should provide a healthy working environment. They need to prioritize the workers' health in choosing office supplies. Some companies are even trying to offer better air quality and safe building materials.

● **구조로 보면**

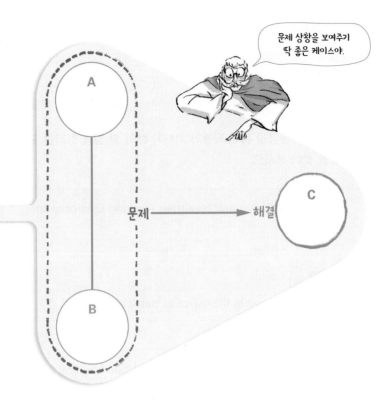

0 각 단락의 내용을 |보기|에서 고르시오.

┤보기├

ⓐ 건강한 업무 환경을 만들기 위한 노력

ⓑ Emma를 통해 경고하고자 하는 메시지

ⓒ Emma가 상징하는 사무직 근무자의 질병과 원인

A _____   B _____   C _____

1 The Work Colleague of the Future 캠페인의 목적을 찾아 쓰시오.

> _____

2 다음은 건강한 업무 환경을 위해 직원과 회사가 해야 할 일을 정리한 표이다. 빈칸에 알맞은 말을 찾아 쓰시오.

Steps for a Better and Healthier Working Environment	
Office Workers	• often _____ positions • take _____ • move in the office as much as possible
Employers	• choose safe _____ • offer better air quality and safe building materials

3 이 글의 요지로 가장 적절한 것은?

① Employers are responsible for the bad health of their employees.

② Emma has bad working habits, leading to her poor shape and ill health.

③ Emma was created by researchers to warn people of dangers in the workplace.

④ We need to pay more attention to working habits and environment not to become Emma.

이 글의 구조를 선택한 이유를 아나?

문제가 주제! 해결책이 요지!

글쓴이가 어떤 현상이나 이슈에 대해 문제를 제기할 때가 있다. 문제를 제기함으로써 그 심각성을 강조하기도 하고, 원인을 분석한 뒤 해결책 또는 대안을 제안하기도 한다. 이런 글의 핵심은 해결책이다. 글쓴이가 글을 쓴 목적이 바로 여기에 있기 때문이다. 제시한 현상에서 주제를 발견했다면, 글쓴이가 어떤 원인을 제거하거나 감소시켜 해결책으로 연결 짓는지에 주목하자. 해결책이 바로 글의 목적이자 글쓴이의 주장이니까.

4 어휘

밑줄 친 ailments와 바꾸어 쓸 수 <u>없는</u> 것은?

These <u>ailments</u> are caused by sitting long hours in a bad position, too much staring at the computer screen, lack of sun rays, or poor air quality in the office.

이 단어를 써서
뭘 말하려는지 알까?

① diseases
② illnesses
③ disorders
④ functions

5 어휘

밑줄 친 still과 동일한 의미로 사용된 것은?

이 문맥에서 쓰인
의미는?

We sit <u>still</u> at our desks too long without moving, and our bodies are impacted by this lifestyle.

① I tried again and <u>still</u> I failed.
② He <u>still</u> lives with his parents.
③ Keep <u>still</u> while I tie your shoe.
④ I <u>still</u> can't remember his name.

Still is used:
① to say that something continues to be possible
② to show that you did not expect something to happen
③ to say that you stand, stay, sit, etc. without moving

poor sleep quality

215 words

★★★☆☆

(A) One of the most common problems many people face nowadays is poor sleep quality. No matter how much sleep we get, we just don't seem to have the energy to tackle the day. I've experienced the same problem, and I'd like to share a simple but effective solution.

(B) Among other things, I stopped misusing caffeine. Caffeine is said to last five to seven hours in our system after consumption. So we've been told not to drink too much caffeine, or else we won't be able to sleep at night.

(C) But did you know that it actually lasts longer than that? In fact, the half-life of caffeine is five to seven hours, so if you drink coffee at 3:00 pm, there's a good chance that 50% of that caffeine is still in your system until 10:00 pm, and a quarter of the original caffeine by 5:00 am the next morning. This can severely disrupt your restorative sleep when a lot of important things are going on in your mind and body such as information processing, creating new ideas, and healing muscle tissues.

(D) So, my advice is ＿＿＿＿＿＿＿＿＿＿＿ so that you still have that morning boost and still get the effect going throughout the day, but not let it disrupt a good night's slumber.

● **구조로 보면**

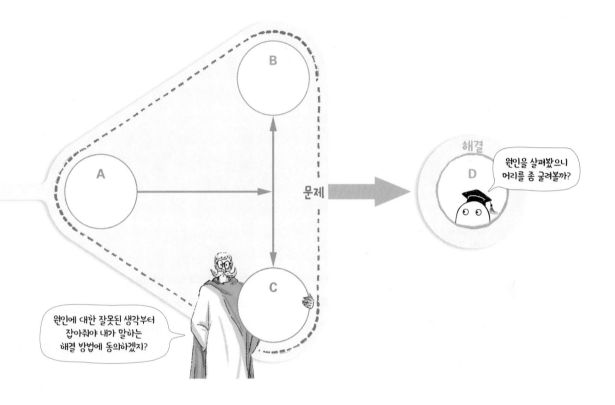

0 각 단락의 역할을 |보기|에서 고르시오.

> | 보기 |
>
> ⓐ 알려진 원인   ⓑ 실제 원인
> ⓒ 문제 제기   ⓓ 해결 방안

A _____   B _____   C _____   D _____

1 이 글의 주제로 가장 적절한 것은?

① how to schedule restorative sleep

② how to improve the quality of sleep

③ how to overcome caffeine addiction

④ how to prolong the effect of caffeine

2 이 글의 내용과 일치하는 것은?

이 글의 구조 속에서
내용 파악했나?

① Morning coffee can disrupt our sleep throughout the night.

② Drinking coffee in the afternoon has little impact on restorative sleep.

③ The effect of caffeine lasts well beyond seven hours after consumption.

④ The best way to overcome sleep deprivation is to stop caffeine consumption.

3 이 글의 흐름으로 보아, 빈칸에 들어갈 말로 가장 적절한 것은?

문제의 원인,
어디에 있는지 알아?

① drink caffeine before noon

② slowly try to cut down on caffeine

③ find an alternative to caffeinated drinks

④ don't stress yourself out with the amount of caffeine intake

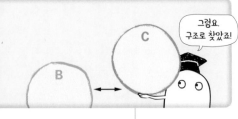

그럼요.
구조로 찾았죠!

4

어휘

밑줄 친 last의 의미와 가장 가까운 것은?

Caffeine is said to <u>last</u> five to seven hours in our system after consumption.

이 문맥 속에서 쓰인 의미를 알아?

① The movie <u>lasted</u> almost three hours.

② She always comes <u>last</u> and leaves first.

③ I saved the <u>last</u> piece of the pie for you.

④ The <u>last</u> time I met him, he looked quite healthy.

5

어법

다음 문장의 흐름으로 보아, 빈칸에 알맞은 말을 |보기|에서 골라 쓰시오.

| 보기 |

who   what time   how hard

(1) No matter _____ he tries to save money, unexpected expenses always seem to pop up.

(2) No matter _____ she talks to, she cannot seem to get a straight answer about what happened.

(3) No matter _____ he goes to bed, he always wakes up early feeling refreshed and energized.

어떤 상황이나 조건이 결과에 영향을 미치지 못할 때 사용하는 'no matter + 의문사'

'no matter + 의문사'는 '어떤 조건이나 상황이 ~하더라도 ...하다'란 뜻을 전할 때 사용하는 접속사야. 조건이나 상황이 결과에 영향을 주지 않을 때 사용하지.

• no matter + how/what/who: '어떻게/무엇이/누가 ~하더라도

No matter how much sleep we get, we just don't seem to have the energy to tackle the day.
잠을 많이 자더라도 기력이 없는 것 같다.

잠의 양이 기력 회복에 영향이 있다는 걸까, 없다는 걸까?

→ 잠의 양이 수면의 질에 영향을 주지 않는다는 의미야. 수면의 질에 영향을 주는 원인은 다른 데 있다는 것을 짐작해볼 수 있어. 실제로 그렇게 전개된 내용을 확인했지?

false hunger

222 words

★★★☆☆

A If you feel hungry an hour after a big meal, it should be false or fake hunger. Craving for food, when you are not really hungry, comes from emotional disturbances like boredom, sadness, and depression. When you want comfort and satisfaction for some reason, eating offers temporary relief from your stressful emotions.

B This habit of eating for emotional reasons goes back to ancient times. At that time, it was a good and healthful strategy because food was extremely scarce. Fatigue and depression were desperate signs that they had to eat anything right away to survive. The problem is that the strategy has been coded in your DNA, even in this age of plenty. Now, too much calorie intake and unhealthy snacks cause many health problems like obesity, diabetes, and a high cholesterol level. Still, we reach for food whenever we feel insecure and stressed as our ancestors did so many years ago.

C Then, how can you overcome false hunger? Awareness and recognition is the first step. When you feel hungry after a nutritiously balanced meal, try to recognize if your hunger is true or false. Pay attention to your feelings and identify the cause of them. When you train yourself with this skill of awareness and recognition, false hunger will appear less frequently, and you will go back to a healthier life.

● **구조로 보면**

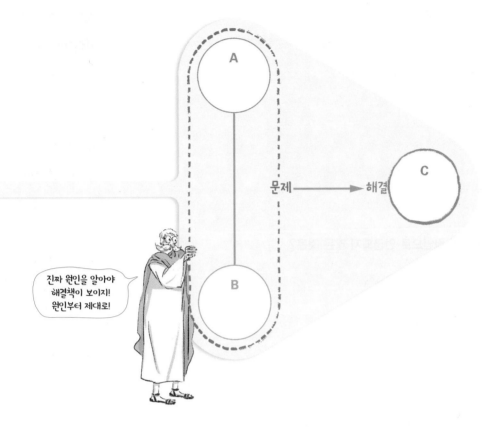

0 **각 단락의 내용을 |보기|에서 고르시오.**

> ┤보기├
>
> ⓐ How can we overcome false hunger?
>
> ⓑ Why is false hunger a problem?
>
> ⓒ What is false hunger?

Ⓐ _____ Ⓑ _____ Ⓒ _____

구조를 보면서
주제를 확인했나?

1 다음 중 의미하는 바가 나머지와 <u>다른</u> 것은?

① false or fake hunger

② craving for food when not hungry

③ eating for emotional reasons

④ a nutritiously balanced meal

2 가짜 배고픔의 원인으로 언급되지 <u>않은</u> 것은?

① 우울함

② 슬픔

③ 스트레스

④ 영양 부족

3 가짜 배고픔이 야기하는 문제와 글쓴이가 제시한 해결책을 우리말로 쓰시오.

문제

해결책

4

밑줄 친 Craving의 의미로 가장 적절한 것은?

> <u>Craving</u> for food, when you are not really hungry, comes from emotional disturbances like boredom, sadness, and depression.

① the act of accepting something
② a way of limiting or stopping something
③ an extremely strong desire for something
④ an act of showing that you will not do something

이 단어들을 사용한 의도를 아나?

5

밑줄 친 relief의 의미로 가장 적절한 것은?

> When you want comfort and satisfaction for some reason, eating offers temporary <u>relief</u> from your stressful emotions.

① a sculpture carved on a surface
② removal of something painful
③ someone who replaces another
④ food or services for people in need

6

밑줄 친 if와 쓰임이 같은 것은?

이 표현을 왜 썼는지 알까?

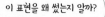

> When you feel hungry after a nutritiously balanced meal, try to recognize <u>if</u> your hunger is true or false.

① She would gladly come <u>if</u> you call her.
② I can't remember <u>if</u> he came to the meeting.
③ We will cancel the picnic <u>if</u> it rains tomorrow.
④ He would have failed <u>if</u> you had not helped him.

6

(A) While many people seek friendship through social media, it can have a damaging effect on its users' psychological well-being.

(B) According to a study, a surprising number of people suffer from jealousy, low self-esteem, and depression as a result of using social media. Researchers have pointed out that "social comparison" causes such undesirable mental conditions.

(C) Looking at others' selfies posted online, you feel that everyone but you seems to have a perfect life. You see them having more fun, meeting exciting people, and looking gorgeous. Everything they do looks better. You become jealous of them. Your self-esteem takes a hit, and you become depressed.

(D) If you feel really bad after using social media, it is a good idea to reduce time online. Also, remember that the online postings are the most memorable moments for your friends. They are supposed to look fantastic. So, stop making comparisons with others. Most of all, we should all remind ourselves that the purpose of social media is to make human connections, not to show off. Showing a sincere human side is the best way to stay truly connected with others.

● 구조로 보면

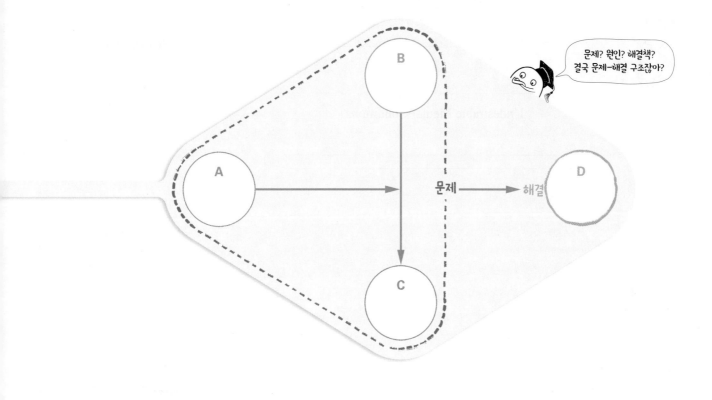

0 단락 A, B, C 의 역할을 | 보기 | 에서 고르시오.

| 보기 |
ⓐ 사례   ⓑ 원인 분석   ⓒ 문제 제기

A _____   B _____   C _____

1 이 글의 내용을 바탕으로 다음 표를 완성하시오.

문제? 해결?
어느 쪽이야?

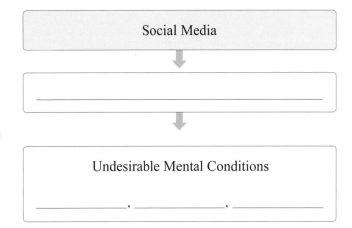

Social Media

⬇

_____

⬇

Undesirable Mental Conditions

_____, _____, _____

2 다음 중 글쓴이와 생각이 <u>다른</u> 사람은?

글쓴이의 생각,
구조로 파악했나?

① Jin: Looking at the picture she posted, Hye-soo had a good time with her family on her birthday. I should congratulate her.

② Min: I need to spend less time on my cell phone and go out to the park and exercise.

③ Pill: The math problem is so hard. I'll post a picture of the question and ask my friends for help.

④ Jung: I can't see the new shoes in the picture because they're covered by my pants. I should take it again and upload it.

정답과 해설 50쪽

3

밑줄 친 표현을 참고하여 빈칸에 들어갈 알맞은 말을 어법에 맞게 쓰시오.

- While many people seek friendship through social media, it can have a damaging <u>effect on</u> its users' psychological well-being.
- According to a study, a surprising number of people <u>suffer from</u> jealousy, low self-esteem, and depression as a result of using social media.
- Showing a sincere human side is the best way to stay truly <u>connected with</u> others.

문맥에 맞게
단어를 사용할 줄 아나?

(1) Recently, over 80% of the workers in the U.S. _____ work-related stress.

(2) It is believed that color has a(n) _____ our moods, feelings, and emotions.

(3) I was able to _____ my new neighbor immediately. We've been good friends ever since.

4

밑줄 친 표현을 참고하여 빈칸에 들어갈 말을 |보기|에서 골라 어법에 맞게 쓰시오.

<u>Looking at others' selfies posted online</u>, you feel that everyone but you seems to have a perfect life.

┤보기├

bring   fly   watch

(1) _____ movies based on novels, people often compare the novel and the film.

(2) _____ at the speed of 1.6 kilometers an hour, mosquitoes find their targets through smell.

(3) Tiny blood vessels run through tunnels in bone tissues, _____ oxygen and nutrients to bone cells.

the nocebo effect

235 words

★★★★★

A We are all familiar with the placebo effect. The placebo effect happens when our symptoms get better, even with fake medicine. The expectation of recovery is enough to trigger a chain of positive reactions in our bodies. Now, the opposite of the placebo effect is the nocebo effect. When people have negative expectations about medication, they can feel side effects. The nocebo effect is a problem because it can _____ the benefits of medication and it interferes with our recovery.

B The nocebo effect can happen by just being informed of the potential side effects of the medication. In New Zealand, the news coverage of a medicine's potential side effects has increased the reports of side-effect cases by 600%. It is also due to the nocebo effect that people blame ordinary, everyday symptoms for their medication. We all have headaches, mild pains, and nausea in our daily lives, and we do not care about them. But with the nocebo effect, we tend to accuse our medication of these symptoms. To avoid the nocebo effect, we should understand what triggers our negative reaction. We should ask ourselves if our minor side effects are genuine ones or just the nocebo effect. Also, you can consider minor side effects as a positive sign that the medication is working effectively in your body. This attitude can change uncomfortable feelings into a promising signal, and it will help you to recover.

● **구조로 보면**

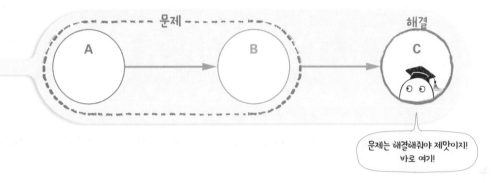

문제는 해결해줘야 제맛이지!
바로 여기!

0 이 글을 세 단락으로 나눌 때, **C** 가 시작되는 첫 두 단어를 네모 안에 쓰시오.

C [   ]

1 이 글의 흐름으로 보아, 빈칸에 들어갈 말로 가장 적절한 것은?

① provide
② reduce
③ obtain
④ enjoy

2 nocebo effect를 일으키는 원인으로 글쓴이가 제시한 것을 모두 고르면?

이 글의 구조에서, 원인이 제시된 단락은?

① 약물의 부작용에 대해 알게 되었을 때
② 두통이나 메스꺼움이 약물 때문이라고 생각할 때
③ 약물의 효능에 대해서 제대로 고지받지 않았을 때
④ 사소한 부작용은 문제가 되지 않는다고 생각할 때

3 이 글의 요지로 가장 적절한 것은?

글쓴이가 해결책을 제시한 이유를 아나?

① We should not mistake the nocebo effect for genuine side effects.
② The nocebo effect and the placebo effect are caused by the same mechanism.
③ Understanding the nocebo effect leads to the beneficial working of medication.
④ Minor symptoms such as headaches and other pains are part of everyday life.

4 <어휘>

밑줄 친 trigger의 의미와 거리가 먼 것은?

The expectation of recovery is enough to <u>trigger</u> a chain of positive reactions in our bodies.

① start
② cause
③ accuse
④ produce

5 <어휘>

단어들의 관계가 나머지와 다른 것은?

① major : minor
② genuine : fake
③ recovery : medication
④ ordinary : extraordinary

6 <어휘>

다음에 제시된 단어들을 포괄하는 단어로 가장 적절한 것은?

headache	mild pain	nausea	weight loss

① cure
② symptom
③ coverage
④ medicine

According to statistics, South Korea is the leader among the countries that have the most cosmetic surgeries per capita. In a 2013 survey, one in five Korean women had cosmetic surgery, [   ] only one in twenty American women had. There can be many possible explanations for this unusual phenomenon. First, in Korea, beauty has economic as well as aesthetic values. In Korea, applicants should submit their resumes with their photos on them. Therefore, applicants cannot but care about their looks. Actually, in many jobs, to look nice is as important as to have good professional skills. Secondly, certain standards of beauty are considered ideal. For example, double eyelids, a small nose, and a V-line chin are typical descriptions of beautiful women. Those who do not have these features are sometimes looked upon as "not being pretty enough." As every woman is not born with these features, many young women have to resort to plastic surgery. In this situation, to accuse women of their craze for cosmetic surgery does not help. Instead of blaming women, we should look into the socioeconomic causes and find more reasonable remedies. For example, the stereotyped beauty standard itself should be changed. Other issues such as the job market standard and the cultural pressure on women should be addressed as well.

● 구조로 보면

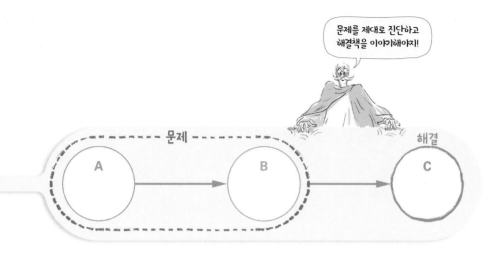

0 이 글을 세 단락으로 나눌 때, 각 단락이 시작되는 부분의 첫 두 단어를 네모 안에 쓰고, 단락의 내용을 |보기|에서 고르시오.

> ┤보기├
>
> ⓐ 현재 상황을 개선하는 방안
>
> ⓑ 한국과 미국 여성의 성형수술 비율 비교
>
> ⓒ 1인당 성형수술 비율이 높은 국가 순서
>
> ⓓ 한국에서 아름다움의 가치와 획일화된 기준

A According to   _____

B   _____

C   _____

1 이 글의 전개 방식으로 적절하지 <u>않은</u> 것은?

① 통계 자료를 사용하여 현상을 객관적으로 제시하고 있다.

② 문제에 대한 원인을 두 가지 측면에서 분석하고 있다.

③ 사례를 대조하여 원인을 분석하고 있다.

④ 문제 해결을 위한 근본적인 방안을 모색하고 있다.

2 이 글의 목적으로 가장 적절한 것은?

문제–해결 구조에서 핵심은 뭐?

① to analyze the stereotypical beauty standards of the modern society

② to look into the social and cultural issues regarding cosmetic surgery

③ to blame women for their ill-advised dependence on cosmetic surgery

④ to criticize the impropriety of recruiting procedures of Korean companies

3 이 글에 가장 어울리는 속담은?

① It never rains but it pours.

② Never leave a stone unturned.

③ A rolling stone gathers no moss.

④ Don't judge a book by its cover.

4

어법

이 글의 흐름으로 보아, [   ]에 들어갈 말로 가장 적절한 것은?

> In a 2013 survey, one in five Korean women had cosmetic surgery, [   ] only one in twenty American women had.

① because
② before
③ while
④ since

5

어휘

이 글에서 사용된 features의 의미로 알맞은 것은?

> For example, double eyelids, a small nose, and a V-line chin are typical descriptions of beautiful women. Those who do not have these <u>features</u> are sometimes looked upon as "not being pretty enough."

문맥으로 정확한 의미를
알 수 있나?

① accessories
② appearances
③ experiences
④ functions

왜 문제해결 구조로 썼을까?

문제 상황으로 몰아넣고 해결책을 제시!

관심을 기울이도록 문제 상황부터 먼저!

문제의 원인 속에서 해결책 제시하기.

이게 내가 문제-해결 구조를 택한 이유!

이 챕터에서는

지문에서	문제는	어떻게 해결되었나?
① wrong posture ⑥ social media	한계	원인을 제거하는 방법으로
② earworm ⑤ false hunger ⑧ cosmetic surgery	현상	원인을 제거하는 방법으로 원인을 감소시키는 방안으로
③ Emma	결핍과 괴리	원인을 감소시키는 방안으로
④ poor sleep quality ⑦ the nocebo effect	오해와 오류	원인을 재정의

다음 글을 읽고, 주어진 문장이 들어가기에 가장 적절한 곳을 고르시오.

> Instead of that, say to them, 'I can't deal with that now but what I can do is I can ask Brian to give you a hand and he should be able to explain them.'

Whenever you say what you can't do, say what you can do. This ends a sentence on a positive note and has a much lower tendency to cause someone to challenge it. (①) Consider this situation — a colleague comes up to you and asks you to look over some figures with them before a meeting they are having tomorrow. (②) You simply say, 'No, I can't deal with this now.' (③) This may then lead to them insisting how important your input is, increasing the pressure on you to give in. (④) Or, 'I can't deal with that now but I can find you in about half an hour when I have finished.' (⑤) Either of these types of responses are better than ending it with a negative.

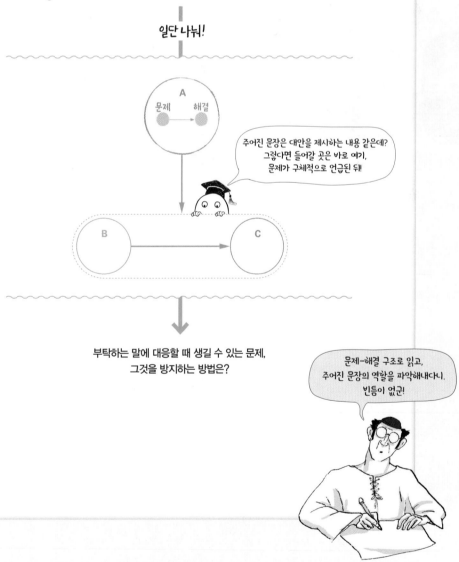

일단 나눠!

A
문제 ● → ● 해결

주어진 문장은 대안을 제시하는 내용 같은데?
그렇다면 들어갈 곳은 바로 여기,
문제가 구체적으로 언급된 뒤!

B → C

부탁하는 말에 대응할 때 생길 수 있는 문제,
그것을 방지하는 방법은?

문제-해결 구조로 읽고,
주어진 문장의 역할을 파악해내다니.
빈틈이 없군!

CHAPTER **05**

NO!

대립

통념을 꺾고! 내 생각을 주장하기!

다음 글을 읽고, 각 네모 안에서 문맥에 맞는 낱말을 고르시오.

School assignments have typically required that students work alone. This emphasis on (A) [collective / individual] productivity reflected an opinion that independence is a necessary factor for success. Having the ability to take care of oneself without depending on others was considered a requirement for everyone. Consequently, teachers in the past (B) [more / less] often arranged group work or encouraged students to acquire teamwork skills. However, since the new millennium, businesses have experienced more global competition that requires improved productivity. This situation has led employers to insist that newcomers to the labor market provide evidence of traditional independence but also interdependence shown through teamwork skills. The challenge for educators is to ensure individual competence in basic skills while (C) [adding / decreasing] learning opportunities that can enable students to also perform well in teams.

*competence: 능력

이 글의 구조에서 제시된 관점과
낱말이 쓰인 문맥이 일치하나?

the fastest
running animal

168 words

★★☆☆☆

(A) People usually believe that the cheetah is the fastest running animal on Earth. However, this is only partially correct. The truth is that there are two fastest running animals on Earth. One is, of course, the cheetah, and the other is the pronghorn antelope in North America.

(B) The cheetah can run at a top speed of 70 miles per hour. The cheetah had better run fast, because in the grasslands of Africa, its natural habitat, it must outrun its prey to catch them. The other fastest animal, the pronghorn antelope, can also run at 70 miles per hour. Interestingly, in North America, the pronghorn antelope, a prey, is the fastest, while in Africa a predator is the fastest. This fact indicates that there must have been a now-vanished predator for the pronghorn antelope to evolve to run so fast.

(C) Therefore, the cheetah and the pronghorn antelope run fast for opposite reasons; one sprints fast to catch its prey, while the other runs fast to escape from its predator.

*pronghorn antelope: 가지뿔영양

● 구조로 보면

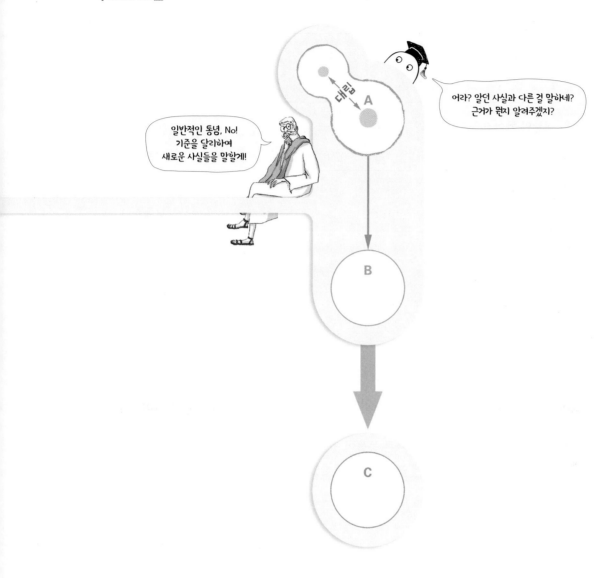

0 각 단락의 역할을 |보기|에서 고르시오.

┤보기├

ⓐ 통념과 반박   ⓑ 문제 제기   ⓒ 근거

ⓓ 해결 방안   ⓔ 결론   ⓕ 원인 분석

Ⓐ _____   Ⓑ _____   Ⓒ _____

1

왜 비교하고 있는지
알까?

다음 물음에 대한 답을 우리말로 쓰시오.

(1) 글쓴이는 어떤 두 대상을 비교하고 있나?

> _____

(2) 두 대상의 공통점은 무엇인가?

> _____

(3) 두 대상의 차이점은 무엇인가?

> _____

2

이 글을 읽고 알 수 없는 것은?

① 치타와 가지뿔영양은 비슷한 속도로 달릴 수 있다.
② 치타는 발 빠른 사냥감을 잡기 위해 빨리 달린다.
③ 포식자뿐 아니라 사냥감도 가장 빠른 동물이 될 수 있다.
④ 가지뿔영양의 빠른 속도 때문에 포식자가 멸종하였다.

3

통념? 반박?
글쓴이의 생각은?

이 글의 제목으로 가장 적절한 것은?

① The Evolution of Animals
② The Two Fastest Animals in the World
③ The Relationship Between Predators and Prey
④ An Ideal Habitat for Animals: Africa or North America

4

어휘

단어들의 관계가 나머지와 다른 것은?

① catch : release
② predator : prey
③ outrun : overtake
④ opposite : similar

5

어법

밑줄 친 one과 the other가 각각 가리키는 것을 찾아 쓰시오.

> Therefore, the cheetah and the pronghorn antelope run fast for opposite reasons; <u>one</u> sprints fast to catch its prey, while <u>the other</u> runs fast to escape from its predator.

• one　　　 : _____

• the other: _____

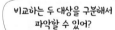

비교하는 두 대상을 구분해서
파악할 수 있어?

6

어법

다음은 어떤 글의 일부이다. 빈칸에 들어갈 알맞은 말을 쓰시오.

> Chronic sleep deficiency often has two consequences. _____ is that it damages our memory and concentration. _____ is that it increases our level of stress hormones and thus leads to a disorder of the body's normal metabolism.

chronic
만성적인
metabolism
신진대사

Silk Road

222 words

★★★☆☆

A
As the "Silk Road" is a well-known term, many people think they know well what it is all about. They assume that the Silk Road is a single road from China to Europe through which Chinese goods, including silk, traveled to the west. (①) However, this understanding is only partially correct.

B
(②) The Silk Road was neither an actual road nor a single route. It was a network of routes used by traders for more than 1,500 years from when the Han dynasty of China opened trade with the West until when the Ottoman Empire blocked trade with the West. (③)

C
It is also important to realize that not only goods traveled along the Silk Road. Silk, porcelain, tea, and spices traveled from the East to the West, and in exchange, horses, glassware, and textiles traveled from the West to the East. (④) But religion, ideas, technologies, and even diseases also spread along the Silk Road. Gunpowder from China changed the very nature of the battle and quickened the fall of the knight class and the rise of the bourgeois. Also, the Plague in the fourteenth century that devastated Europe and caused the collapse of the Middle Age order is believed to have spread from the East to Europe.

● **구조로 보면**

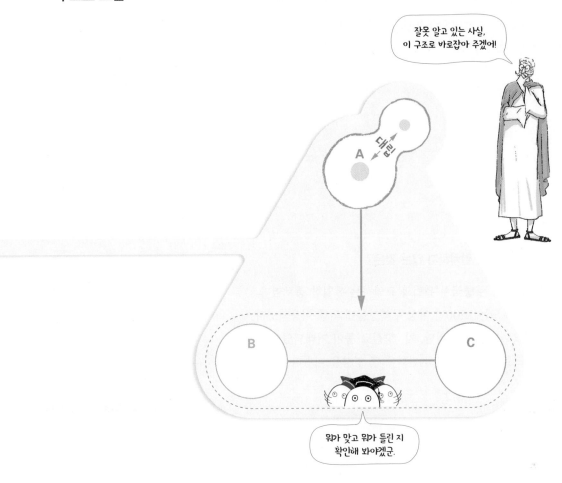

0 각 단락의 내용을 |보기|에서 고르시오.

> ┤보기├
>
> ⓐ Silk Road란 무엇인가
>
> ⓑ Silk Road를 통한 교역과 그 영향
>
> ⓒ Silk Road에 대한 사람들의 부정확한 이해

A _____ B _____ C _____

1

대립 구조 속에서, 이 문장의 역할을 아나?

이 글의 흐름으로 보아, 다음 문장이 들어갈 가장 적절한 곳은?

> Some historians preferred the term "Silk Routes" because it better reflects the various paths used by traders.

①   ②   ③   ④

2

이 글의 내용과 일치하지 않는 것은?

① 실크로드는 중국이 유럽과 교역하는 유일한 통로였다.
② 실크로드는 1500년 이상 무역상들에 의해 이용되었다.
③ 실크로드를 통해 비단, 차, 향신료 등이 거래되었다.
④ 실크로드는 서양 사회 변화에 큰 영향을 미쳤다.

3

이 글의 제목으로 가장 적절한 것은?

① The History of the Silk Road
② The Actual Truth about the Silk Road
③ The Economic Value of the Silk Road
④ The Impact of the Silk Road on Social Change

이 글을 쓴 목적, 구조에서 보여?

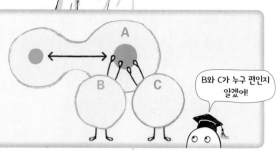

B와 C가 누구 편인지 알겠어!

어휘

4 밑줄 친 partially의 의미로 가장 적절한 것은?

> However, this understanding is only <u>partially</u> correct.

이 문장의 의도를 알까?

① in every possible way
② in a general or basic way
③ somewhat but not completely
④ according to a very strict explanation

어휘

5 밑줄 친 devastated와 바꾸어 쓸 수 <u>없는</u> 것은?

> The Plague in the fourteenth century that <u>devastated</u> Europe and caused the collapse of the Middle Age order is believed to have spread from the East to Europe.

① ruined
② destroyed
③ preserved
④ overwhelmed

어법

6 빈칸에 알맞은 표현을 │보기│에서 골라 쓰시오.

│ 보기 │
neither ~ nor   not only ~ but also

neither A nor B
A도 B도 아닌(동시 부정)
not only A but also B
A뿐 아니라 B도(B를 강조)

(1) By analyzing a political cartoon, readers can learn _____ about social issues _____ about the historical background on which the cartoon is based.

내용의 흐름을 보고 있나?

(2) I _____ enjoy watching TV _____ playing video games, so I often spend my free time reading books or going for a walk.

the Palace of
Versailles

215 words

(A) The Palace of Versailles is regarded as one of the most luxurious and artistic palaces in the world. However, it was also once one of the dirtiest places because it did not have toilets when it was first built.

(B) Versailles was a small town near Paris and did not have a sewage system when the construction of the palace began. Therefore, toilets could not be built inside the palace. In place of toilets, the royal family used their private pots, and some visitors brought their own pots to use as toilets. (①) However, servants and other visitors had to find corners, hallways, and gardens of the palace to use as their toilets. (②) As a result, the palace looked ___(A)___ but smelled ___(B)___ . (③) The problem became so serious that Louis XIV ordered that the palace hallways be cleaned every week. (④)

(C) In 1768, after 144 years of its construction, the palace finally began to add toilets to its buildings. It is ironic that a necessity such as a toilet was not on the architect's priority list, while much more care was given to the construction of luxury facilities such as the opera house and ballrooms.

● **구조로 보면**

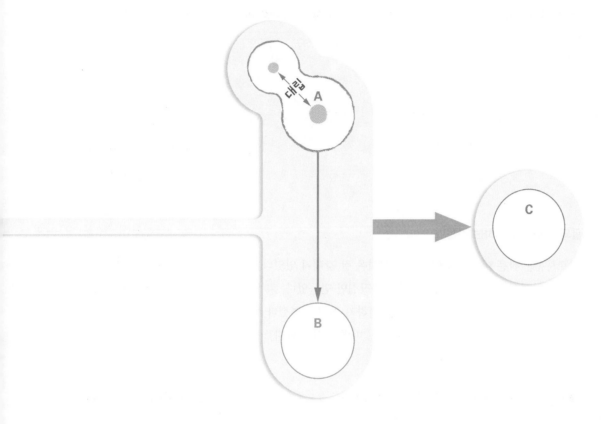

0 **각 단락의 역할을 |보기|에서 고르시오.**

| 보기 |

ⓐ 통념과 반박   ⓑ 문제 제기   ⓒ 근거   ⓓ 결론

Ⓐ _____   Ⓑ _____   Ⓒ _____

1 이 글의 흐름으로 보아, 다음 문장이 들어갈 가장 적절한 곳은?

이 문장의 역할을 보여주는
시그널을 아나?

> The king also placed a sign, or an "etiquette," which originally meant "keep off the grass" to forbid people from entering the gardens.

①   ②   ③   ④

2 이 글의 내용과 일치하는 것은?

① 베르사유는 작은 마을이었지만 하수 시설은 잘 갖춰져 있었다.
② 베르사유 궁전을 건립할 때 왕실 전용 화장실만 만들었다.
③ 루이 14세는 궁전 내 지독한 냄새를 해결하기 위해 노력했다.
④ 베르사유 궁전에는 지금도 화장실 시설이 마련돼 있지 않다.

3 이 글의 제목으로 가장 적절한 것은?

이 글을 쓴 목적,
구조로 확인했나?

① Etiquette at Versailles
② The History of Versailles
③ Versailles: Its Grandeur and Magnificence
④ One of the Best-kept Secrets of Versailles

통념에 이어 흐름을 반전시키는 연결어가 나왔다면, 다음은 주장이 나올 차례

글쓴이가 사람들이 일반적으로 알고 있거나 당연하다고 생각하는 사실이나 믿음을 먼저 제시한 뒤, 흐름을 반전시키는 연결어를 사용했다면 이어지는 내용에 주목해야 한다. 잘못된 통념을 반박하거나 사람들이 미처 알지 못하는 사실을 언급하기 때문이다. 그것이 바로 글쓴이가 주장하는 바이자 글을 쓴 목적이다.

• 통념을 제시하겠다는 신호: We[They/People] think[believe/regard/assume] that ~
                            / ~ be regarded as ~
• 반박을 예고하는 신호: however[yet/still] / partially ~ / the truth is ~

4

어휘

이 글의 흐름으로 보아, (A)와 (B)에 들어갈 말로 알맞게 짝지어진 것은?

> As a result, the palace looked [(A)] but smelled [(B)] .

이 글의 핵심 내용을
한 문장으로 표현하면?

	(A)		(B)
①	clean	·········	sweet
②	ugly	·········	strange
③	old	·········	pleasant
④	beautiful	·········	awful

5

어휘

밑줄 친 necessity와 luxury facilities의 의미를 비교해 보고, 각자의 삶에서 necessity에 해당하는 것이 무엇인지 우리말로 쓰시오.

> It is ironic that a <u>necessity</u> such as a toilet was not on the architect's priority list, while much more care was given to the construction of <u>luxury facilities</u> such as the opera house and ballrooms.

necessity:
items that are essential
to our lives

luxury:
something that you like
having but do not need

> _____

virtual reality

186 words

★★★☆☆

(A) Many people regard virtual reality (VR) only as an interesting toy because they usually encounter VR in games on a PC or in virtual reality experiences of famous tourist spots.

(B) However, the development of VR technology is rapidly changing the real world. For example, VR is enabling doctors to exercise difficult operations before they perform real operations. In Singapore, doctors used a VR tool to prepare for a difficult operation to separate Siamese twins. The operation was a huge success. For another example, automakers are using VR in crash tests. This is not only 98% accurate, but it also saves a lot of money because no real vehicles are actually destroyed in the tests. Architects are also using VR technology to build virtual model homes. Through VR model homes, buyers can understand better what it would be like to live in the actual homes. Also, VR homes are far cheaper to build than real model homes. Thus, VR homes are becoming one of the most important marketing tools. In this way, VR is already changing our real lives at the forefront of the development of technologies.

● **구조로 보면**

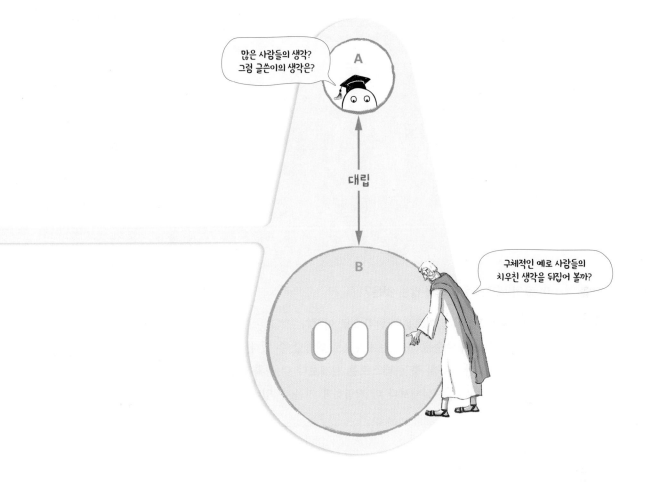

O **각 단락의 내용을 |보기|에서 고르시오.**

┤보기├

ⓐ VR의 발달 과정

ⓑ VR의 실생활 적용 사례

ⓒ VR에 대한 일반 사람들의 인식

ⓓ VR에 흥미를 느끼는 사람들의 특징

Ⓐ _____ Ⓑ _____

1 밑줄 친 부분의 근거로 제시한 것 세 가지를 찾아 우리말로 쓰시오.

* _____

* _____

* _____

사람들의 인식을 뒤집는 내용,
파악했어?

2 이 글의 내용과 일치하지 <u>않는</u> 것은?

① 사람들은 VR을 흥미로운 장난감으로 여긴다.
② 의사들은 실제 수술을 하기 전에 VR로 연습할 수 있다.
③ VR을 이용한 자동차 충돌 테스트는 실제보다 더 정확하다.
④ VR 모델 하우스는 실제보다 더 저렴하게 지을 수 있다.

3 이 글의 제목으로 가장 적절한 것은?

① The Role of VR in the Game Industry
② The Growing Use of VR in Real Life
③ The Economic Value of VR in Industry
④ The Various Kinds of VR Used in Vehicles

어휘

4

이 글의 흐름으로 보아, 빈칸에 들어갈 말로 적절하지 <u>않은</u> 것은?

Many people _____ virtual reality (VR) only as an interesting toy, because they usually encounter VR in games on a PC or in virtual reality experiences of famous tourist spots.

대립 구조에서 통념을 말하는 시그널, 알까?

① treat

② think

③ enable

④ consider

어휘

5

밑줄 친 forefront의 의미로 가장 적절한 것은?

접두사 **fore-**: ~앞에, ~전에
forehead 이마
forecast 예측하다

VR is already changing our real lives at the <u>forefront</u> of the development of technologies.

① an earlier date

② the hidden place

③ the extreme front

④ the opposite of up front

5

Alaska

220 words

★★★★☆

(A) Alaska was a cold, barren, frozen land inhabited by Inuit and other peoples before Russia took it over in the mid-eighteenth century. As the land was worthless to them, Russia first approached the United States to sell the land. So, when William Seward, US Secretary of State, purchased Alaska from Russia, people called the deal "Seward's folly." They laughed at Seward for his foolishness to spend so much money on the cold, worthless land. The Senate approved the deal on the first vote. There were 37 votes in favor and 2 against.

(B) However, _____ . After the US bought Alaska, much gold was discovered. People rushed to Alaska to become rich, and Alaska prospered. After that, crude oil, the modern "gold," was found in Alaska. The oil is now transported across the country through pipelines, and Alaska's oil has become one of the main resources of America. In case other resources should be found in Alaska's unexplored parts, the worth of Alaska would increase more.

(C) But for "Seward's folly," the US would have lost the most profitable deal in history. Seward bought Alaska for just $7.2 million in 1867. How much would Alaska be worth today? It is estimated that Alaska would be worth $15 trillion today, almost 2080 times its original price!

● **구조로 보면**

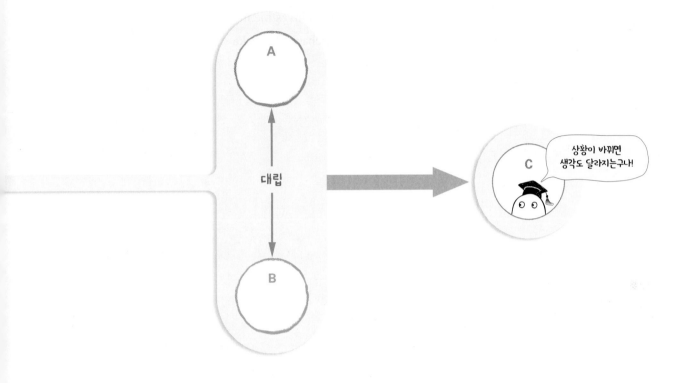

상황이 바뀌면
생각도 달라지는구나!

0 **이 글의 전개 방식으로 적절하지 않은 것은?**

① 알래스카 구매 당시 사람들의 인식을 언급하고 있다.
② 알래스카 개발 과정을 상세히 설명하고 있다.
③ 사람들의 인식이 바뀌게 된 계기를 제시하고 있다.
④ 알래스카의 현재 가치를 평가하고 있다.

1 **이 글의 흐름으로 보아, 빈칸에 들어갈 말로 가장 적절한 것은?**

① Seward should not have bought the polar bear land

② American people did not accept the Senate's decision

③ Alaska, "Seward's Icebox" proved to be a good investment

④ the American Congress voted against the purchase of Alaska

2 **이 글의 제목으로 가장 적절한 것은?**

① The US Senate's Wise Decision

② The History of Alaska and Russia

③ Undiscovered Treasures of Alaska

④ Foolish Purchase Turned Into Large Profit

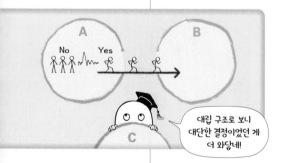

정답과 해설 66쪽

어법

3

빈칸에 들어갈 말로 적절한 것은?

이 문장의 의도 파악했나?

_____ "Seward's folly," the US would have lost the most profitable deal in history.

① After
② Above
③ Without
④ Because

실제 있었던 일을 반대로 가정, 그에 따른 결과를 생각해 볼 때 사용하는 But for

실제는 그렇지 않았는데, 뒤바뀔 수도 있던 과거의 일로 표현해서 실제 있었던 일의 의미를 되짚어 볼 때, but for 또는 without을 사용할 수 있어. 이때, 결과를 표현하는 절에 '조동사+현재완료'를 사용하기 때문에 if절이 없더라도 동사를 보고 문맥의 의도를 알 수 있지. 중요한 건, 가정법으로 글쓴이의 생각을 표현한다는 점!

But for "Seward's folly," the US would have lost the most profitable deal in history.
(= If it had not been for "Seward's folly," ~) – 가정법 과거완료

→ (그때 당시) Seward's folly가 없었더라면 미국은 역사상 가장 수익성 있는 거래를 놓쳤을 거라는 가정을 통해 그만큼 엄청난 거래였음을 강조.

어휘

4

알래스카 구매에 대한 사람들의 인식 변화를 나타낸 표현을 찾아 쓰시오.

Before	After
_____	_____

the battle of
Salamis

198 words

★★★★☆

(A) The most famous battle in the second Persian War between Greek city-states and the Persian Empire is the Spartan 300 soldier's heroic struggle against a huge Persian army at Thermopylae. Yet, as the Spartan 300 all died and the battle was lost, the Battle of Thermopylae was not the battle that saved Greek city-states.

(B) The most crucial point of the second Persian War was the Battle of Salamis. The battle was fought in the straits of Salamis in 480 BC. Before the battle of Salamis, Greek city-states were in great danger because the huge Persian army was advancing towards them. The Greeks were afraid of the relentless Persian advance, so they were fleeing helplessly.

(C) _____, the Athenian general Themistocles persuaded the Greeks to face the Persian fleet at Salamis. Themistocles drew the huge numbers of the Persian fleet into the narrow straits of Salamis. In the narrow sea, the massive number of Persian ships could not move well and became disorganized. The Greek fleet seized this opportunity and won a decisive victory. After the defeat, the Persian Emperor realized that his chance of victory was fast disappearing, so he ordered a retreat. The Battle of Salamis saved Greece!

● 구조로 보면

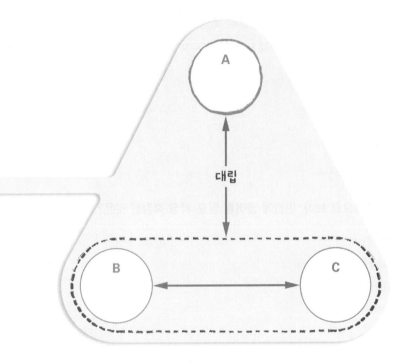

0 각 단락의 내용을 |보기|에서 고르시오.

┌─|보기|─────────────────────────────┐
│ ⓐ 살라미스 전투 과정 및 결과   │
│ ⓑ 제2차 페르시아 전쟁에서 가장 유명한 전투   │
│ ⓒ 제2차 페르시아 전쟁에서 가장 결정적인 전투   │
└──────────────────────────────────┘

A _____   B _____   C _____

1

이 글의 내용과 일치하지 <u>않는</u> 것은?

① 살라미스 전투는 제2차 페르시아 전쟁에서 가장 유명한 전투이다.
② 테미스토클레스가 그리스인들을 설득하여 살라미스 전투를 주도하였다.
③ 살라미스의 좁은 지형을 이용하여 페르시아의 함대를 물리쳤다.
④ 살라미스 전투 패배 후 페르시아 황제는 퇴각을 명령했다.

2

단락을 나눈 의도를 아나?

이 글의 흐름으로 보아, 빈칸에 들어갈 말로 가장 적절한 것은?

① However
② Therefore
③ Otherwise
④ Furthermore

3

글쓴이가 밑줄 친 부분과 같이 판단한 이유 2가지를 우리말로 쓰시오.

• _____

• _____

4

글쓴이가 이 글의 구조로 말하고 있는 것은?

이 글의 제목으로 가장 적절한 것은?

① The Battle that Saved Greece
② The Superiority of the Greek Navy
③ The Importance of a Naval Strategy
④ The Heroic Struggle of Spartan Soldiers

어휘

5 각각의 의미에 해당하는 단어를 |보기|에서 골라 쓰시오.

| 보기 |

advance decisive flee

helpless relentless seize

(1) to move forward _____

(2) to take hold of suddenly _____

(3) to run away from danger _____

(4) not lessening in severity _____

(5) not protected, not able to defend yourself _____

(6) very important for the final result of a particular situation _____

어휘

6 밑줄 친 **drew**의 의미와 가장 가까운 것은?

Themistocles <u>drew</u> the huge numbers of the Persian fleet into the narrow straits of Salamis.

이 단어가 어떤 의도로 쓰였는지 문맥에서 파악할 수 있어?

① traced
② painted
③ deduced
④ attracted

7

Millennials and
Gen Z

229 words

★★★★★

Ⓐ There's been a common misconception that both the Millennials and Generation Z, or simply Gen Z, are essentially the same. But, that would be an oversimplification. The first apparent difference is the age. Born between about 1980 and 1995, the oldest Millennials were in college when the Internet came out. Gen Z, born roughly between 1996 and 2012, grew up with all kinds of information flooding in with its oldest members first learning about social media when they were in middle school. Many people think that Millennials have always had social media, but _____ . The fact is the internet was coming of age alongside Millennials. And it was not in the form of social media— it was email. Gen Z, on the other hand, got their first smartphone when they were very young and prefer enjoying entertainment through online media than the traditional outlets. For them, online media is a place where they can make real connections through direct messages, sharing posts, memes, and videos. While the Millennials are also tech-savvy and dependent on technology, Gen Z seems to have a natural bond with technology.

Ⓓ It is true that both groups are considered "young adults," and are highly connected to the internet and technology. However, a closer look reveals that these generations differ in their attitudes toward money, technology, purchase habits, social media, and career motivations.

● **구조로 보면**

0 이 글을 네 단락으로 나눌 때, **B**와 **C**가 시작되는 부분의 첫 두 단어를 네모 안에 쓰시오.

B

C

1 이 글의 제목으로 가장 적절한 것은?

① Millennials vs. Gen Z: How Are They Different?

② Millennials vs. Gen Z: Why Misconception Persists

③ Millennials or Gen Z: Which One Are You and What Does It Mean?

④ Defining Generations: Where Millennials End and Generation Z Begins

2 이 글의 흐름으로 보아, 빈칸에 들어갈 말로 가장 적절한 것은?

구조로 내용을 이해했나?

① this is completely false

② this remains to be seen

③ they are not as easily persuaded

④ there is much truth to this claim

3 이 글의 내용과 일치하는 것은?

① The youngest Millennials did not have access to the internet until they reached adulthood.

② Millennials do not seek meaningful relationships through social media as much as Gen Z.

③ Online connectivity became even more intense even before Gen Z was born.

④ Other than the age gap Millennials and Generation Z share basically an identical outlook on life.

어휘

4 인터넷 등장 시기와 두 세대의 차이점을 고려해볼 때, 밑줄 친 the traditional outlets에 해당하는 예를 우리말로 쓰시오.

> The fact is the internet was coming of age alongside Millennials. And it was not in the form of social media—it was email. Gen Z, on the other hand, got their first smartphone when they were very young and prefer enjoying entertainment through online media than <u>the traditional outlets</u>.

> _____

어법 · 어휘

5 다음 중 빈칸에 들어갈 알맞은 말을 어법에 맞게 쓰시오.

두 대상을 비교할 때
• differ in + 속성
• differ from + 대상

| differ in | differ from |

(1) The east and west coasts of Canada _____ climate.

(2) I can tell the twins apart—they _____ height.

(3) Can you explain how this smartphone _____ that one?

(4) This recipe _____ that one because it doesn't require eggs.

문맥에 맞게 표현을 사용할 줄 알아?

8

Louisa May Alcott
192 words
★★★★

Louisa May Alcott is best known for her novel *Little Women*, the story of a family in nineteenth-century America. At first sight, *Little Women* appears to talk about traditional themes such as family values, sacrifice, and self-control. A closer look, however, reveals a deeper social message in the story. Alcott was a strong believer in women's rights and a strong opponent against slavery, and Alcott's voice is reflected in Josephine March, the second oldest daughter of the March family. Unlike her traditionally feminine sisters, she uses a male nickname, "Jo," ▢(A)▢ chooses to become a writer, a profession for males in her day. Jo even wishes to join the Union Army to fight against slavery. However, Jo is not always sure of herself; Jo has the ambition to succeed as a writer, and supports herself through her writing, ▢(B)▢ she also strongly feels the pressure to act as a dutiful daughter and follow traditional values. Alcott intentionally put more weight on Jo's words and actions than those of her more feminine sisters; Jo represents Alcott's views on social issues, and Jo's character reflects Alcott's understanding of women's dilemma in the nineteenth century.

*Union Army: (남북 전쟁 때의) 북부군

● 구조로 보면

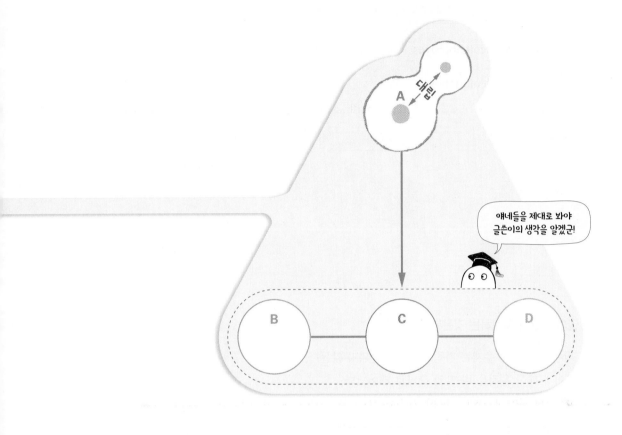

0 이 글을 네 단락으로 나눌 때, 각 단락이 시작되는 부분의 첫 두 단어를 네모 안에 쓰고, 단락의 내용을 |보기|에서 고르시오.

┤ 보기 ├
ⓐ 소설 속 인물이 겪는 갈등
ⓑ 인물에 반영된 작가 올컷의 의도
ⓒ 올컷의 사상과 소설 속 인물
ⓓ 올컷의 소설과 소설이 전하는 메시지

A Louisa May _____

B _____

C _____

D _____

1 루이자 메이 올컷이 '작은 아씨들'을 통해 전달하고자 하는 메시지이다. 빈칸에 알맞은 말을 찾아 쓰시오.

Alcott's Social Message

(1) Louisa May Alcott approves _____ .

(2) Louisa May Alcott opposes _____ .

2 이 글의 내용과 일치하는 것은?

① '작은 아씨들'의 주제는 가족애에만 국한되지 않는다.
② 루이자 메이 올컷은 네 딸의 장녀로 태어났다.
③ '조'는 다른 자매들과는 달리 매우 여성적이었다.
④ 루이자 메이 올컷은 작품에서 딸들을 균등하게 다루었다.

3 이 글의 제목으로 가장 적절한 것은?

① The Creative Process of *Little Women*
② Beneath the Surface: The Underlying Theme of *Little Women*
③ How *Little Women* Influenced the Women's Rights Movement
④ Writer's Block: How Louisa May Alcott Overcame the Obstacles

대립 구조를 통해
글쓴이가 말하려는 것은?

4

어법

이 글의 흐름으로 보아, (A)와 (B)에 들어갈 말로 알맞게 짝지어진 것은?

> Unlike her traditionally feminine sisters, she uses a male nickname, "Jo," ____(A)____ chooses to become a writer, a profession for males in her day.
>
> – 중략 –
>
> However, Jo is not always sure of herself; Jo has the ambition to succeed as a writer, and supports herself through her writing, ____(B)____ she also strongly feels the pressure to act as a dutiful daughter and follow traditional values.

빈칸 앞뒤 내용의 관계를 파악했나?

	(A)		(B)
①	or	⋯⋯	yet
②	yet	⋯⋯	so
③	and	⋯⋯	yet
④	but	⋯⋯	for

5

어휘

밑줄 친 represents의 의미로 가장 적절한 것은?

> Jo represents Alcott's views on social issues, and Jo's character reflects Alcott's understanding of women's dilemma in the nineteenth century.

① to show that something exists or is true

② to put something where people can see it

③ to find out who someone is or what something is

④ to act or speak officially for someone or something

왜 대립 구조로 썼을까?

통념을 꺾고!
내 생각을 주장하기!

일반적인 통념을 먼저,

NO! 내 생각은 달라!

탄탄한 근거로 멋들어지게 설득하기!

이게 내가 대립 구조를 선택한 이유!

이 챕터에서는

지문에서	무엇을	어떻게 주장하고 있나?
① the fastest running animal	상식	다른 기준과 관점으로 반박
② Silk Road ⑦ Millennials and Gen Z	흔한 오해	객관적인 설명으로 반박
③ the Palace of Versailles ④ virtual reality ⑥ the battle of Salamis ⑧ Louisa May Alcott	치우친 인식	객관적인 설명과 분석 내용으로 반박
⑤ Alaska	시대적 통념	역사적 사례로 반박

다음 글을 읽고, 각 네모 안에서 문맥에 맞는 낱말을 고르시오.

School assignments have typically required that students work alone. This emphasis on (A) collective / individual productivity reflected an opinion that independence is a necessary factor for success. Having the ability to take care of oneself without depending on others was considered a requirement for everyone. Consequently, teachers in the past (B) more / less often arranged group work or encouraged students to acquire teamwork skills. However, since the new millennium, businesses have experienced more global competition that requires improved productivity. This situation has led employers to insist that newcomers to the labor market provide evidence of traditional independence but also interdependence shown through teamwork skills. The challenge for educators is to ensure individual competence in basic skills while (C) adding / decreasing learning opportunities that can enable students to also perform well in teams.

*competence: 능력

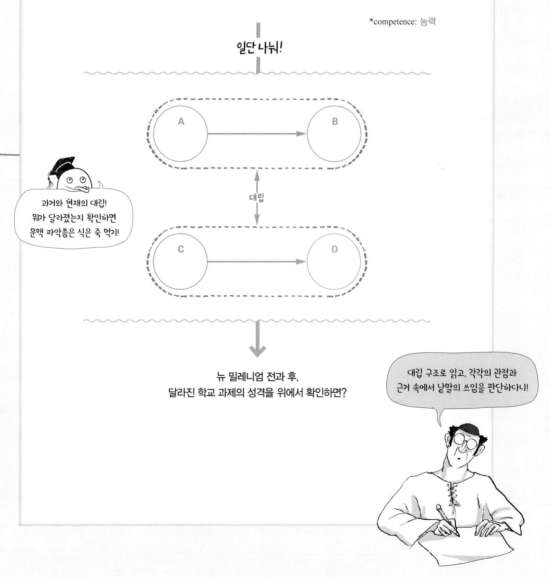

일단 나눠!

과거와 현재의 대립!
뭐가 달라졌는지 확인하면
문맥 파악쯤은 식은 죽 먹기!

대립

뉴 밀레니엄 전과 후.
달라진 학교 과제의 성격을 위에서 확인하면?

대립 구조로 읽고, 각각의 관점과
근거 속에서 낱말의 쓰임을 판단하다니!